G000068381

Sea Angling
in Southern England

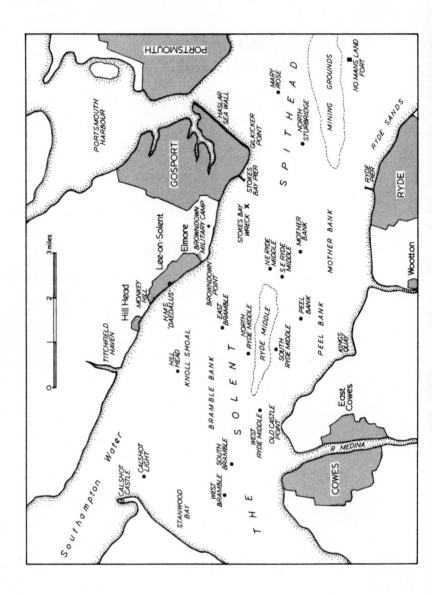

Sea Angling
in Southern England

Peter Smith

DAVID & CHARLES
Newton Abbot   London   North Pomfret (Vt)

British Library Cataloguing in Publication Data

Smith, Peter
   Sea angling in southern England.
   1. Salt-water fishing – England
   I. Title
   799.1'6'09422   SH457

ISBN 07153 8172 5

Library of Congress Catalog Card Number 80–85504

Photoset by Typesetters (Birmingham) Ltd
and printed in Great Britain
by Butler and Tanner Ltd, London and Frome
for David & Charles (Publishers) Limited
Brunel House   Newton Abbot   Devon

Published in the United States of America
by David & Charles Inc
North Pomfret   Vermont 05053   USA

Contents

Introduction

Along the approximately 200 miles of coastline spanning Dorset, Hampshire and the Isle of Wight and Sussex the sea angler is treated to as wide a variety of species of fish as anywhere in Britain. The aim of this book is to give the angler a picture of what fishing is available from boats and along the beaches, and where and how he can best go out and enjoy it.

One of the sport's greatest attractions is its surprise element: the good day's catch which materialises from nothing, and the rotten blank that comes when everything should have gone right. Despite this, the well-founded experiences of anglers over the years have set patterns, established fishing marks, and proved that certain techniques work. It is their experiences that I have tapped, together with my own years of angling, to produce this book. Its foundation is that if I've tried it myself and it works, and if anglers I've talked to have put it to good regular use, then I've included it as a feature anglers can expect to bring them results. I am hopeful that you can turn to any kind of sea angling along the Dorset, Hampshire and Isle of Wight and Sussex coastline and find here the guidelines that long experience has shown do work.

In years of running a sea-angling column in *The News* at Portsmouth, many thousands of anglers have nattered to me about their catches. Where their experiences can be useful to others, their ideas are here.

Lest any angler should doubt the wealth of good fish that are out there to be caught, the section of the book analysing specimen catches from this stretch of sea over the years should give pretty sound reassurance. I am greatly indebted to Mike North, President of the Wessex Division of the National Federation of Sea Anglers and the Federation's honorary fish recorder from 1971 to 1976. Together we spent many hours analysing the specimen catches to produce an informed overall picture of the fishing in the area – a study never made in this form before.

While I have aimed to cover charter-boat fishing, small-dinghy fishing and beach and rock fishing, together with pier techniques, I have deliberately not covered the specialized aspect of sea angling in harbours and river estuaries. Dorset, Hampshire, the Isle of Wight, and Sussex have a rich abundance of fishing in their harbours and estuaries, so much so that the techniques are sufficiently varied and specialized to have warranted almost a separate book on their own. Rather than scratch the surface of the topic and fail to do it justice, it seemed more satisfactory to leave it to another day.

As far as possible I have tried to keep the book up to date, but sea anglers will know only too well the fast-changing nature of the sea, fishing trends, and even natural and man-made landmarks. Not even I can stop the demolition gangs knocking down landmark chimneys used by anglers, or stop nature shifting sandbanks or changing the habits of fish species. At least I hope that armed with this mixture of well-tried angling experiences you can turn to any kind of sea angling in the south with a fair idea of what fish you can expect, where best you can find them, and how best you can catch them.

1 Sea Angling in the South

Sea angling today plays a greater part in the lives of more people than ever before in Britain, a nation finding itself with ever more time on its hands. As a sport it is big business nowadays. A variety of associated industries exists supporting thousands of people so that ever-increasing numbers of sea anglers can enjoy their sport. There are the manufacturers of rods, reels, tackle, clothing and equipment; tackle dealers selling the gear; professional bait diggers; a whole section of the boat industry geared to providing fishing boats to suit a great range of requirements; marine chandlers; together with professional skippers, boatmen and an entire charter-boat industry.

One of the richest sections of Britain's natural coastline heritage is the central southern stretch of the English Channel encompassing the shorelines of the counties of Dorset, Hampshire and the Isle of Wight and Sussex. In effect, the coastline is one huge potential fishing ground consisting of 200 miles of fishable beaches and many hundreds of square miles of sea rich in a huge variety of fish − with at least 37 species caught regularly, together with a smattering of rare visitors who occasionally stumble their way up-Channel from normally warmer climes. Every aspect of sea angling − its varied techniques and methods − can be practised along this stretch of coastline and sea. There are deep-water areas and wrecks, inshore rock patches and every kind of seabed attracting different species for boat anglers. Beaches range from rocky headlands to mud, sand and shingle expanses where shore anglers can catch the exceptional conger or the humble flounder. The area boasts numerous piers, sea walls, breakwaters or groynes, and for the harbour and estuary specialist there are at least nine harbours and rivers where the mullet, flatfish and bass can be chased.

This massive potential is augmented by the equally good fishing offered by the neighbouring areas – Lyme Bay stretches further west than Lyme Regis into the renowned west country fishing grounds, and at the other end of the Channel, Rye is a stepping-off point towards the famous Dungeness cod and whiting beaches and boat marks.

With so much on offer for the sea angler, it is no surprise that the catchment area from which anglers are drawn to the central southern coast is enormous.

There are two types of anglers: those who live along the coast and who develop over years of experience a deep local knowledge of their own marks are what you might call the 'locals'; while the increasing numbers of people flocking down from the inland areas as far north as London are what might be termed the 'visitors'.

The large London overspill areas around Reading, Guildford and Camberley are easily linked with the south coast ports and an increasingly large number of clubs are springing up inland, whose members take charter trips in this area. Some of the south coast's biggest beach festivals attract shore anglers from these inland clubs and the days when sea angling was the exclusive sport of those living on the coast are long gone.

It is no doubt the promise of catching large numbers of most species of sea fish together with many top specimens (the area boasts quite a large number of British record or former record fish) that draws the anglers. Club parties travel to the south coast so often that many of their members are fast becoming fine sea anglers able to match the skills of the 'locals'.

While the sport element in sea angling will always remain the prime motivation of the thousands who flock to the coast, go afloat and participate, the value of fish as a food is growing almost daily. Behind the sport there is an increasing feeling of 'freezer' fishing as an added incentive. Most species caught in this area are excellent foods – and in the case of cod, plaice or sole, the sea angler is catching himself an expensive delicacy. There is every indication that fish is going to become more and more expensive in the shops, which will indirectly add to the achievement of catching your own fish.

Central southern England boasts opportunities for three categories of sea angling, which are: (1) going afloat in charter boats for deep-sea angling; (2) going afloat in small boats for inshore fishing; (3) fishing ashore along the hundreds of miles of beaches or from piers.

Charter fleets have built up in the area where the very best fishing is found, and the charterers chase different species according to where they are prominent. Many of these specialities are famous. Littlehampton is renowned for its black bream during the summer. The Isle of Wight and West Solent fleets take tremendous cod catches off the famous Needles marks. Further east, the East Solent fleets take large cod catches in the Nab Tower grounds. Shoreham, Newhaven and Brighton Marina boats are famous for cod catches in winter with the added bonus of having good fishing all the year round.

In the west the Weymouth boats have the tremendous fishing grounds off the Shambles and the marks off Portland Bill.

All the charter fleets have a common bonus in the many wrecks that lie off the coast. Throughout history the English Channel has grown a reputation as a graveyard of ships, with gales taking their toll, with wars adding their casualties, and with the sheer volume of shipping using the Channel guaranteeing collisions so that wrecks will always abound. It is true that central southern England's tides are stronger than those encountered in the west country, where wrecking is at its very best, but wreck trips still provide a wealth of big fish throughout the area, when the problems created by the tides can be overcome.

Another branch of sea angling which was at one time thought to be the exclusive province of the west country – shark fishing – has become an added attraction in the south. Many charter boats now run shark trips to the grounds south of the Isle of Wight – where British record porbeagles were once taken and, more recently, where record threshers have been taken. It is not surprising that with this wealth of angling to be tapped there are nearly a dozen charter fleets spread along the south, with many coastal towns running small-scale charter trips.

For most anglers the only way of reaching deep-water marks – and that means big fish – is to use the charter boats, and for visitors from inland the only way of getting afloat at all is on the charters. There are thousands of anglers, however – mostly locals – who get afloat in their own small boats. The entire coastline of central southern England is rich in fishing accessible to the small-boat angler, from the extreme west in Lyme Bay, round Portland Bill (famous for bass and pollack) to Weymouth Bay, Poole Bay, the Solent, the waters surrounding the Isle of Wight, Spithead and the area inside the Nab Tower, Selsey Bill, the rich black bream and whiting grounds off Littlehampton, the all-the-year-round attractions of Shoreham, Worthing and Newhaven, the bass fishing around Beachy Head, the boat potential off Eastbourne and Hastings, and the nearness of Rye to the cod grounds off Dungeness.

One result is that hundreds of sea-angling clubs thrive in the area, most of which run boat matches regularly, some weekly, ensuring that thousands of small boats are afloat each weekend in the best seasons. In addition, there are hundreds more anglers who fish privately in dinghies, with an increasing trend for individuals to buy larger boats enabling them to forage further afield into the grounds where once only charter boats steamed.

An extension of the benefits of individual clubs to the sea angler is the wealth of interest and assistance available from the National Federation of Sea Anglers. Most clubs are affiliated to the NFSA which is divided into geographical divisions. Hampshire and Dorset together form part of the Wessex Division. Sussex forms the Southern Division and the Isle of Wight has its own. The strength of the NFSA is that it brings together all sea anglers and all clubs under a common umbrella set of rules, creating a standard against which all can measure up. What is more important – especially in the modern age of intense activity on the sea – the NFSA acts as a national collective voice protecting the interests of anglers. This is no mean achievement. When a large container terminal was proposed at Portland, the Wessex Division of the NFSA battled against it on behalf of anglers as it would cause untold damage to the fishing and marine environment. It was due to the voice of the NFSA – far stronger than any number of anglers individually – that the proposal was scrapped.

Individual anglers who do not want to belong to clubs but who would enjoy the benefits of the NFSA can become personal members. Their monetary subscriptions are their way of wishing to assist the Federation in its work, while at the same time enjoying the benefits in return. It is in the field of competitions that the NFSA has the greatest effect on the angler. All affiliated clubs run their matches according to its rules, and specimen sizes are regulated by the Federation.

Recently, the former Honorary Fish Recorder, Mike North, devised and introduced a regionalised specimen award scheme. Before that date, some areas abounding in mature specimens were naturally taking huge proportions of that species' medals, while areas where that particular fish was rare, received none. Under the new scheme, the country is divided into regions, each with its own specimen sizes, drawn up according to past records, and able to be reviewed should trends differ in future. This method was only introduced late in the seventies and in its first years of operation it seems to have been welcomed as a much fairer system.

Throughout the south coast, in addition to a full calendar of angling competitions individually arranged by each club and open only to members of that club, there are a number of open matches – for which anyone may enter. Two of the largest are the Southern TV sea-angling championships and the Wessex Division Champion of Champions competition. For ten years the Southern championships were run with just a break in 1975 and 1976. There are about 300 clubs in the area on the Southern list which enter their champions into the regional heats along the south coast. The two winners from each heat then go to the 'glamour' final at an exotic fishing venue (Shetlands, Orkneys, Hebrides or Ireland) where the winner becomes the champion.

When Southern TV cancelled the event in 1975 the Wessex Division stepped in and laid on a similar contest with heats along the south coast and with an 'exotic' final in Cornwall. This was such a success that it was repeated in 1976. The south-coast angler now has the good fortune of having both competitions running each year, Southern TV having reintroduced its contest, while the Wessex championships are continuing. Having travelled and fished in the Orkneys, Shetlands, Hebrides, Isle of Skye and Cornwall in more than a dozen of these, covering them for my paper, I can vouch for them as being truly memorable occasions.

In addition there are dozens of major open festivals held along the south coast every year, some in boats and some from the shore.

A major attraction of beach angling is that any beach is free to be fished by anyone. No licences or permits are required. The cost of owning, maintaining or hiring a boat is not incurred. It is simply a matter of transporting yourself to a beach – and casting out. And in the south, variety is the keyword. In Dorset rocky headlands can be found where conger, pollack and wrasse are taken. Flatfish abound throughout the area, particularly along the Solent and Sussex shorelines.

Isle of Wight beaches are famous for a huge variety of fish, including regular catches of rays, some huge conger and tremendous bass. Further east, the bass catches from Selsey Bill to Beachy Head are splendid, and further east still you can take cod to go with the flatfish.

The most famous attraction of all is Chesil Beach in Dorset, where shore anglers can cast into deep water off a sharply shelving beach, where mixed bags are taken, including hauls of cod, shoals of dogfish and pout and packs of spur-dogs and ray.

Pier fishing in the south is hardly spectacular and few of the south's piers are renowned for regular big catches, but there are more than a dozen in the area from which fishing is permitted, and which yield plenty of small fish. Especially good fishing can be expected from Hastings Pier – where cod may be caught, mighty plaice are hooked, and which is considered good enough for a major European festival to be held there. Most of the others produce small pollack, whiting, pout and flatfish. Pier fishing is probably the only form of sea angling where you must ascertain before you start that angling is permitted. Some piers have no restrictions, others have partial restrictions, and some ban fishing completely.

About the only other bar to angling from the beaches is that imposed by large numbers of holiday-makers. The south coast attracts some of the largest holiday crowds in the whole of Britain. Hastings, Brighton, Eastbourne, Southsea, Bournemouth, the Isle of Wight and Weymouth are world famous for their holiday crowds. They often make daytime beach angling completely impossible. It is only right and fair that everyone should have equal usage of a national heritage such as the coastline, and beach anglers must make allowances for the crowds. If it is impossible to find a remote, empty beach it is better not to fish at all, rather than run the risk of causing injury. Remember that flying weights and hooks can be lethal during casting. One saving grace in this problem is that evening fishing from the same beaches that are crowded by day is often more profitable, as well as safer.

Harbours and estuaries provide some of the most intense sea angling along the south coast, and local knowledge is crucial to success. It is more often the locals who spend a great deal of time exploring their harbours and creeks where the top flatfish and bass catches often materialise. Throughout the south there are at least nine harbours fished regularly in one of the most popular usages of very small dinghies. For safety reasons, harbours often provide the only waters sheltered enough for small dinghies to be used. Once again, the considerations of other water users must be kept firmly in mind. Swimmers, water skiers, yachtsmen and pleasure-cruiser boatmen all have equal rights to use harbours and nowadays their numbers are increasing. This problem becomes particularly acute in some harbours like Langstone, Chichester and Poole where some of the best bass runs are in the entrances – which are the very busiest areas for boat traffic.

So, what can you expect to catch? Charter boats will put you among the biggest fish, which are the thresher and porbeagle sharks. Boats fishing the deep-water marks produce congers, any of the three regular species of rays caught – thornback (which is the most common), small-eyed (or painted), and spotted (or homelyns) – and other big fish. These are cod, pollack (becoming more prevalent in Hampshire waters), bull huss, spur-dog, smoothhound and tope. Occasionally the deep-water marks produce big monkfish, angler fish and turbot along the coast.

Smaller fish are taken in larger numbers and provide most of the sport for charter anglers and small-boat fishermen. These include black bream (taken in large numbers), pout (omnipresent), whiting (attractive when shoaling heavily in winter), dogfish (taken in vast numbers), mackerel (widespread in summer), bass (including many fine specimens), and scad and garfish in lesser numbers.

Flatfish are taken both in dinghies and off the beaches, with flounders being the most numerous. Plaice, dabs and sole are plentiful, with brill and turbot being rarer. Silver eels and mullet are taken in harbours, and the area is occasionally visited by strangers. Among the latter are the trigger fish or file fish (including a former British record or two), red bream from some wrecks, and even sea trout and salmon from some of the estuaries and harbours.

Southern England holds plenty of its own bait sources so that the main baits used both afloat and ashore can be obtained by anglers themselves. Throughout the area ragworm and lugworm can be dug, although constant over-digging has reduced the stock of worms available, and the digging is harder nowadays. For those who fish for bass or aim for large flatfish there are supplies of peeler crab in rocky areas. Slipper limpet, cockles, mussels, and other shellfish are plentiful, though not so often used as the worms.

Afloat, anglers can usually catch enough of their own mackerel in summer to use as bait for that season's fish, and freeze them down for use as bait in winter. Most fish caught afloat will feed on mackerel – large pieces for tope, conger and skate, thin strips for whiting, bream and dogfish. The great exception to the rule of anglers obtaining their own bait is the squid, which is a very common bait but has to be bought. Californian squid are most popular, being particularly killing for cod in the Nab Tower and Needles grounds, and when used in thin strips for bream right along the south coast. Sandeels, which are netted in several of the harbours, provide excellent bait when used live for bass, while hermit crabs, which can be a menace when fishing, make useful baits for a variety of species, especially smoothhounds in summer.

A deeper feeling of satisfaction can be obtained from sea angling if you have gathered your own bait, for that in itself – bait digging effectively, or netting sandeels, or even catching mackerel to order – is an art. But there are occasions when it is impossible to find time to get bait, and then you must buy it. Not surprisingly, bait supplying is a full-scale business in the south. Most tackle dealers offer a live worm-bait service – dependent upon tide cycles and tide times. Many of them stock frozen mackerel and squid, and many carry artificial baits such as lures, spinners and feathers.

Most charter boats include the cost of bait in the hire price for the day, or failing that provide the bait on board as an extra. With so many anglers seeking the available bait it is always wise to book your bait requirements in advance in order to avoid disappointment.

The happiest feature of sea angling where bait is concerned is that you need never despair. If you have failed to get your own worms, and if all shops are out of stock, there is always natural bait on the beaches. Slipper limpet litter most beaches, especially after a blow, and there are some anglers who visit beaches deliberately relying on slipper limpet alone. Similarly, peeler crab can be found on beaches if the angler knows where to look. Mussel banks, cockle beds and razorfish, available at low tide, all provide good natural bait sources.

2 The Fish

It is no idle boast that the coastline of central southern England offers some of the finest fishing anywhere in Britain. The only way to substantiate such a claim is by analysing the catches of the anglers in the area compared with the rest of the country. Difficulties in achieving this arise because not all anglers record their catches − not even top quality fish − and, especially in the case of freelance anglers not belonging to clubs, no one ever hears of their catches.

There is only one comprehensive record of all known top quality fish, and that is the one kept by the National Federation of Sea Anglers. The Federation set down a minimum specimen-size weight for each species of fish, at one time recognised throughout the country but since the mid 1970s changed to a regionalised basis. Any angler in each region must achieve the appropriate minimum weight before he has caught a fish officially recognised as a 'specimen'. Specimen fish are rare and many anglers fish a whole life-time without catching one.

Guardian of the specimen lists until the 1976/1977 season was the Federation's former Honorary Fish Recorder, Mike North, who is now the President of the Wessex Division. He kindly gave me access to his records of 11,000 registered specimens from 1,600 clubs throughout Britain up to 1976 (before the regionalisation scheme was introduced), and my analysis of them shows some remarkable features about central southern England.

Similar comparisons have become impossible since the introduction of the regionalised system as each region now has its own standards, and there is no way of comparing the south's catches against a national specimen standard size. There is every reason to believe, however, that the trends illustrated by the analysis of the mid 1970s (seen here for the first time) are just as applicable today.

18

Undoubtedly the best fishing in Britain for sole, sting ray, smoothhound, monkfish, spur-dog, blonde rays, and three-bearded rockling is in this area, which provides more than 80 per cent of all the specimens in Britain for these species. The area is among the best for big tope, cod, brill, and pout fishing, contributing more than 60 per cent of their specimens. More than half the specimen congers, small-eyed rays, black bream, angler fish and silver eels in Britain come from the south, and it is the strength in depth which makes the area so remarkable. A third of all the country's specimen plaice, whiting and thornbacks come from the south as does more than a quarter of the country's specimen flounders, turbot, mackerel and red bream, together with more than a fifth of all specimen grey mullet, bull huss and pollack.

Within the overall area of the south, the separate counties of Dorset, Hampshire and Sussex have clear hunting grounds for different species. Hampshire produced all the specimen smoothhounds in Britain in 1974 and 1976, for example, and more than 60 per cent of all the sting rays in the country in the mid 1970s. Dorset produced the only beach-caught specimen red bream in 1976, every specimen red mullet in 1975 and every specimen boat-caught grey mullet in the same year. With many species, the large numbers of specimens reflect the large numbers generally taken in the area. But not always. In the case of cod, for example, Hampshire and Sussex have produced a large number of specimen cod – but few cod come from the area. The south-eastern corner of Britain and East Anglia produce huge numbers of codling and yet far fewer big cod.

The records also reveal trends developing over the years and the fishing movements through the area. For example, boat anglers in the south took more than 60 per cent of all boat-caught specimen cod in Britain in 1974, the same again in 1975, but in 1976, the last year that the figures are available, figures slumped to less than a third of the country's total. Again, in 1974, when the Shambles Bank in Dorset was fishing well, more than 80 per cent of all Britain's blonde ray specimens came from this area. It had dropped to just two blondes out of eight in 1975 and down to one specimen blonde in the entire area in 1976. Black bream best illustrate the movement of fish through an area as shown by the specimen records. In late spring and early summer the majority of the south's specimens were being caught. But during late summer and autumn the west country anglers were taking all the specimens, with just an occasional fish coming from the south.

The following is my analysis of all the main species caught in the south, their identification, distribution, quantity and quality. The tables produced for each species represent the percentage of all the specimens in Britain to come from the south divided into three categories: (1) boat and beach combined; (2) boat-caught specimens; (3) beach-caught specimens. The tables are compiled from the data extracted from the specimen records of the National Federation of Sea Anglers up to 1976.

Sole

Dover sole are the most commonly caught of the soles in the south (the other variations being extremely rare). There is no mistaking the sole as its shape is unique among the flatfish, being an elongated oval elliptical fish. It is usually very dark brown or sepia and sometimes mottled. Central southern England enjoys the best sole fishing in the country. A 1lb 8oz sole is a good fish.

Table 1

Specimen sole in southern England

	1976	1975	1974
Beach and boat combined	56%	80%	72%
Boat caught	12½%	68%	52%
Beach caught	66%	89%	83%

Hampshire alone provided more than half the specimen sole in 1975 as the following table shows:

Table 2

Specimen sole in Hampshire

	1976	1975	1974
Beach and boat combined	—	55%	47%
Boat caught	—	44%	30%
Beach caught	18%	63%	56%

Sole are taken over a variety of grounds ranging from soft mud, soft sand, to occasionally quite rough ground. The main baits used for sole are worms, with lugworm being favourite in Sussex (where 21 per cent of all Britain's beach-caught specimens were taken in 1976). Sole fishing from boats demands that the bait is kept moving and a sliding leger is effective. Baited spoons are not essential. One aspect of the sole is that it feeds better by night than by day. It is taken most often during autumn, between July and October.

Plaice

Plaice are prolific throughout the south, being easily recognised by the prominent orange spots on their dark skin. Further identification features are that the skin is smooth, and there are no prickles on the lateral line on the top of the fish.

Plaice like sandy, shingly, clean grounds, and there are famous plaice marks dotted throughout the south – Poole Harbour which has produced giants over 7lb; Hastings Pier, where specimen fish are often taken; and sandy areas like Spithead and Hayling Bay.

The south regularly provides about a third of all the specimen plaice in Britain, and a 3lb plaice is a good'un.

Table 3

Specimen plaice in southern England

	1976	1975
Beach and boat combined	29%	33%
Boat caught	23%	—
Beach caught	38%	60%

Although plaice feed mainly on molluscs, anglers achieve greatest success with worm bait. In Hampshire, which produced just over a quarter of all specimen beach-caught plaice in 1975, ragworm is favourite, while further east in Sussex (which accounted for 23 per cent of beach-caught specimens in 1976) lugworm is preferred. Anglers prepared to experiment with peeler crabs should be rewarded with the best, if fewer, fish. Plaice feed mostly by day, and legering or float fishing a baited spoon are the two preferred methods. February to May are the best months for plaice but they are taken through the year in lesser numbers until November.

Flounders

These are probably the most prolific flatfish in the south, liking muddy and sandy bottoms, and frequenting harbours, estuaries, river mouths and sandy beaches. Hampshire produces the best big flounder fishing of the three counties in the south. The flounder is usually olive green or brown in colour and can be recognised by running your finger along its lateral line from the tail to the head, where you will find a prominent row of prickles. Although large numbers are taken in the south, the area produces only about a quarter of all the specimens. You can be proud of any flounder over 2lb.

Table 4

Specimen flounders in southern England

	1976	1975
Beach and boat combined	18%	28%
Boat caught	7%	27%
Beach caught	21%	28%

Because flounders are able to live in fresh water they give an added dimension to the angler who can fish for them in the lower reaches of rivers. Flounders like brackish water and their diet includes crabs. Anglers taking small flounders on worm bait could often pick out fewer but bigger flounders by changing to peeler crabs. The baited spoon method is particularly killing for flounders, the visible attraction of the spoon being most effective against this species.

Dabs

Dabs are probably far more abundant than anglers realise and if more people fished specifically for them, results would be pleasantly surprising. Most anglers fish harbours for flounders and plaice; if they fish outside in the open sea, they are usually after bigger species. Few people choose the open sea fishing trips to hunt dabs, but they abound in the south in large numbers. Dabs are recognised mainly by their rough sand-papery skin. They are brown and freckled and have a small mouth. A 1lb dab is a good catch.

Table 5

Specimen dabs in southern England

	1976	1975
Beach and boat combined	15%	20%
Boat caught	16%	15%
Beach caught	13%	21%

Worm bait is usually used for dabs, with ragworm being favourite in Hampshire and lugworm the tops in Sussex. Dabs like sandy ground and leger tackle is preferred. Baited spoons are not so effective against dabs.

Cod

Big cod are the favourite quarry of the vast majority of winter boat anglers in the south. Nearly every boat that goes afloat then is after cod – and the south boasts some of the finest big cod fishing in the country. In January 1977 on successive weekends, charter skippers contacted me with three cod – 25lb, 31lb 3oz, and 34lb 12oz – typical of the pattern for the main Hampshire cod areas, the Nab Tower and Needles marks. In 1979 I reported several catches of cod over 40lb from the Needles area during a boom year, which rivalled the bonanza period of the early 1960s.

Table 6

Specimen cod in southern England

	1976	1975	1974
Beach and boat combined	29%	48%	41%
Boat caught	32½%	63%	62%
Beach caught	20%	12%	15%

Hampshire and Sussex are the two favourite counties for cod, with Shoreham and Newhaven among the Sussex hot spots. Cod have huge cavernous mouths and will eat anything – sprats, any small fish, crabs, shellfish and worms – and they feed largely by sight. For this reason, a white bait – squid – is preferable and is most often used in Hampshire. Black lugworm are favoured in Sussex, especially for beach cod fishing. Taking the visual aspect of bait a step further, many anglers use a white spoon to provide attraction on their cod tackle.

Pout

A member of the cod family, this poor relation is much smaller and infests the south coast in vast numbers, always providing sport when everything else stops feeding, and often being cursed by anglers when shoals of tiny pout nibble away at a big bait aimed for a larger fish. When pout are first caught they have a copper colouring with vertical cross-bands, but soon after capture they fade and become a dirty brown and white.

While the south produces pout by the thousands to annoy anglers, it is also a top area for big pout. In 1976, a good year, the south produced more than three quarters of all the boat-caught specimens in Britain and nearly two thirds of all specimens in the country. You can be pleased with any pout over 1lb 8oz.

Table 7

Specimen pout in southern England

	1976	1975
Beach and boat combined	63%	25%
Boat caught	77%	36%
Beach caught	48%	19%

Pout are the true scavengers of the seabed and will feed on anything offered − even pout strip. They feed anywhere − on rocks, over sand, in harbours, off piers and jetties and over wrecks.

Whiting

The other very common member of the family is the whiting, which is a winter fish only in the south and which used to be taken in huge numbers. I have taken them three-at-a-time on three-hook paternoster gear a few years back − but they are not as plentiful nowadays. Like pout, they feed on a great range of baits, with fish strip being the favourite. About a third of all specimen whiting in Britain fall to anglers in the south. Again, anything over 1lb 8oz is a good fish.

Table 8

Specimen whiting in southern England

	1976	1975
Beach and boat combined	34%	33%
Boat caught	34%	42%
Beach caught	33%	13%

Pollack

In 1976 a long run of big pollack developed in Hampshire waters, which was an unusual occurrence for these fish of the same family as the cod, pout and whiting. This new trend now seems to be a permanent feature. Pollack are found on wrecks and over rocky ground, with deep water attracting the big fish over 20lb and with shallow water holding the small pollack often taken by beach and pier anglers. They feed on small fish and sandeels, and artificial sandeels, red gills, or fish strip baits take them regularly.

There was a 100 per cent increase in the numbers of specimen pollack taken from boats in southern England in 1976 compared to 1975.

Table 9

Specimen pollack in southern England

	1976	1975
Beach and boat combined	21%	15%
Boat caught	20%	10%
Beach caught	24%	34%

The shark family in the south embraces the tope, the smoothhound (two species) and the spur-dog.

Tope

This truly magnificent shark-like fish has two main identifying features. It has shark-like teeth and it has no spots at all. It has a flattish snout, a grey-coloured body and a near-white belly. Boat fishing for tope in the south, especially through Sussex and Hampshire and off Portland, is among the best in the country, and nearly three quarters of all boat-caught specimens in 1976 came from this area.

Table 10

Specimen tope in southern England

	1976	1975
Beach and boat combined	56%	50%
Boat caught	70%	54%
Beach caught	—	—

Tope run to over 70lb but any fish over 35lb is good. Tope bear young and if they can be spared when carrying young, so much the better. Although this species can be eaten, their flesh is rather muscular and tough unless meticulous cooking care is taken. It was the Chinese who put the tope to its best culinary purpose — for the making of shark-fin soup which is in fact tope. Fresh mackerel is the best possible bait in the south, although tope feed naturally on any small fish. Small flatfish make good tope baits if the angler wants to experiment.

Smoothhound

There are two species of smoothhound — the spotted smooth-hound (*mustelus asterias*) which is the common fish most often caught in the south, and the plain smoothhound (*mustelus mustelus*) which is very rare. For identification purposes, the smoothhound is easily recognised by the fact that it has no teeth (despite being a member of the shark family) but hardened lips instead, and by being liberally sprinkled with white spots on its grey skin.

Southern England offers among the best smoothhound fishing in the country, with the only specimens recorded in the mid 1970s — three in 1974 and one in 1976 — coming from the south. It feeds on crabs and shellfish. Hermit crabs are the champion bait for the fish, of which a 12lb or bigger fish is a beauty.

The rarer plain smoothhound is recognisable by having no teeth and no spots. Apart from the difference in the mouth, it looks similar to the tope.

Spur-dog

This species has no teeth, is a darker grey than the tope and can be easily distinguished by a large single spine in front of each dorsal fin. Beware of how you handle the fish or it could inflict a nasty wound with those spines. Big spur-dogs run well in the south, especially from boat marks in Hampshire and Sussex. An eight-pounder is a good fish.

Table 11

Specimen spur-dogs in southern England

	1976	1975
Beach and boat combined	59%	71%
Boat caught	59%	73%
Beach caught	66%	50%

Almost half of all the boat-caught specimens in 1975 were taken off Sussex, while exactly half the British specimens caught from the beach were taken in Dorset.

Spur-dogs, the commercially fished 'dog' providing the country's supplies of 'rock salmon' and 'dutch eel', move through southern waters, being caught off Sussex in February and March and not reaching Dorset until June and July.

Monkfish

This member of the shark family is nearly always taken by accident in the south by anglers chasing rays and generally after mixed fishing. They run very big, with most monks taken in the south exceeding 35lb.

Table 12

Specimen monkfish in southern England

	1976	1975	1974
Beach and boat combined	71%	40%	60%
Boat caught	83%	50%	75%
Beach caught	—	—	—

This strange-looking fish is a cross between a shark (the tail half) and a skate (the front half) − the name monk being derived from mongrel. It hugs any sandy gravelly bottom where it lies partly submerged and feeds on small fish. Any specimen from 35lb upwards is good and they run as high as 70lb. Monkfish tail is a delicacy tasting as good as scampi.

Two fish frequently caught in the south and related to the shark family are the lesser spotted dogfish and the bull huss or nurse hound.

Bull Huss

This is the bigger brother which runs up to 15lb, and which is covered in larger spots and blotches. The south provides about a third of all Britain's specimens, with boat fishing from Sussex the best hunting ground of all.

Table 13

Specimen bull huss in southern England

	1976	1975
Beach and boat combined	23%	15%
Boat caught	37%	31%
Beach caught	8%	—

Lesser Spotted Dogfish

Rather like the pout, dogfish feed over most kinds of ground at all times of the year and will feed on anything. There are sometimes identification difficulties between a large dogfish and a small bull huss – these can be easily solved by looking at the mouth. In the dogfish the nasal flap is joined and almost part of the mouth; with the bull huss, the nasal flap is completely separated from the mouth. Thousands of lesser spotted dogfish are caught in the south, but there is no specimen size listed in the NFSA records.

Skates and Rays

Both are members of the same family, the skates being the big brothers (common skate or bottle-nosed skate) which can run up to 200lb, while the rays are the smaller relatives. The present British record bottle-nosed skate is a 76lb fish from off the Needles, Isle of Wight.

A massive proportion of the rays caught along the south are of three species – thornback, small-eyed or spotted, although two other species – the sting ray and the blonde ray, are also famous in the south and spectacularly high proportions of all specimens of these two fish come from this area. The three main types of ray are quite different in appearance, and although there has been a traditional confusion over identification of rays, there shouldn't really be any trouble.

Thornback Ray

The thornback is basically diamond shaped, mainly brown with dots, spots and a marbled colouring effect over its topside. Its main recognition points are its curved spines all over its wings and in ridges along its tail and upper body.

Thornbacks like sandy shingly ground and are about the first species to break the February deadlock when all is quiet. They can be taken all the year round in this area. Their main diet is small fish, sandeels and crustaceans and the best bait for them is mackerel strip or hermit crab. Ragworm will often take small thornbacks. Big thornbacks run over the 20lb mark but any fish over 12lb is a good ray. The south accounts for just over a third of all the British specimens, with boat fishing being by far the most productive method.

Table 14

Specimen thornbacks in southern England

	1976	1975
Beach and boat combined	35%	26%
Boat caught	41%	26%
Beach caught	8%	20%

Small-eyed Rays

These are also called painted rays. They are greyish with large white spots on the wings, and after being caught white lines begin to appear on the wings, parallel to the leading and trailing edges. They are nearly as numerous as the thornbacks but are slightly smaller, with a 10lb fish being a good catch. Two hot spots for this species are the beaches of south-west Isle of Wight and boat marks off Selsey in Sussex. Boat fishing in the south accounts for more than half of all the specimens taken in Britain.

Table 15

Specimen small-eyed rays in southern England

	1976	1975
Beach and boat combined	35½%	—
Boat caught	55%	—
Beach caught	30%	—

Spotted Rays

This also has an alternative name, the homelyn ray, and is frequently caught in the south, being a smaller fish altogether with 3lb being about the average size. This is another species for which the NFSA does not produce a specimen size. It is easily distinguishable by having distinct small black spots on a brownish-coloured topside – but the spots do not reach the edges of the wings, where the fish appears to have a clear spot-free border. Its skin is smooth, save for some prickles confined to the leading edge of the wing. It lives over sand, and feeds on crabs. Spotted rays will take fish strip or worms.

Sting Ray

Southern England boasts some of the best sting-ray fishing in the country and Hampshire is a hot spot within the south. This ray – which runs to 50lb – has a smooth skin, is rounded in shape, a dirty grey or olive brown in colour, and carries a sting (a sharp spur) in its tail which it can whip over and thus inflict a nasty wound. In 1976 I wrote in my column about an angler off Sussex who caught a sting ray and received just such a wound in the finger, which eventually had to be amputated after infection set in. The south almost had a monopoly of the specimens among its boat anglers in 1976.

Table 16

Specimen sting ray in southern England

	1976	1975	1974
Beach and boat combined	77%	61%	80%
Boat caught	90%	66%	80%
Beach caught	33%	50%	—

Hampshire is a special hunting ground for big sting ray,

especially in the West Solent where the mainland New Forest shore between Sowley and Lepe and the waters off the beach there are a favourite spot.

Table 17

Specimen sting ray in Hampshire

	1976	1975	1974
Beach and boat combined	61%	38%	60%
Boat caught	70%	33%	60%
Beach caught	33%	50%	—

May, June, July and August are the top months for stingers, which feed on worm and crab. Ragworm is a killing bait.

Blonde Rays

In the mid 1960s and early 1970s when the Shambles Bank off Weymouth was in its heyday, the blonde rays were the second favourite fish on the bank after the turbot. Since the Shambles has deteriorated, the number of big blondes, specimens included, has dropped sharply. Blonde rays are prickled all over their surface, are basically fawn or brown with large creamy spots and small dots all over their upper surfaces, right to the edges (in contrast to the spotted rays). They run to over 30lb.

In 1974, 83 per cent of all the blonde ray specimens in Britain came from the south with 75 per cent of all Britain's specimens coming from the Shambles. In 1975 there were just two specimens from the Shambles and in 1976 the only specimen came from Sussex.

There are other rays to be found in the south but these are very rare. The undulate ray is a beautifully patterned fish with black lines all over, each edged meticulously with white spots. One surprise undulate took a happy angler to the finals of the Wessex Division Champion of Champions contest when it popped up out of the blue off Poole, weighing 16lb. The others are even rarer. The cuckoo ray has a single unmistakeable black and yellow spot in the centre of each wing; the starry ray is found more to the north; the eagle ray has a predominant snout and distinctly pointed wings. The British record eagle ray was a 52lb fish taken off the Nab Tower area of Hampshire.

Bass

A fabulous fighting fish which is the favourite with many anglers. When a bass comes aboard it is a solid silver slab, with bristling sharp-spined fins. Anglers in the south are the luckiest in the country for the bass lives predominantly on the south coast and, in fact, nearly half of all Britain's specimen bass come from the central south. A 6lb bass is a beauty. Any double-figure bass is a sea angler's dream.

Table 18

Specimen bass in southern England

	1976	1975
Beach and boat combined	44%	46%
Boat caught	47%	46%
Beach caught	42%	46%

Bass are taken equally well from boat and beach marks in the south where they feed mainly on small fish, sandeels, crabs and worms. The best baits are live sandeel, fish strips, live prawns, squid, peeler crabs, and worms. Whole live pout are good for really big bass. Bass arrive in March and April and last through to October – with many of the biggest fish coming later in the year, particularly during September. In the form of shoal bass, school bass, 'chequers', or whatever their dialectic name, small bass can be caught in great quantity when they shoal in large numbers for safety.

Bass are a statutorily protected fish. In 1976 a commercial fishing minimum size was laid down at 10¼in and on 1 January 1977 the NFSA imposed a minimum 15in size limit on anglers. These limits were imposed when it was feared that the species could be wiped out by being commercially exploited too heavily. In the summer, harbours and estuaries are alive with small schoolies, and they must be put back when caught.

Two of Britain's finest big bass spots are Portland Bill (both for the shore fishing from rocks on the Bill itself and from boats in the Portland Race) and Beachy Head in Sussex.

(*above*) Haslar sea wall, Gosport: the sloping wall gives anglers good access
to fairly deep water within casting range. At low tide the sea washes against
the wall. The skyline of Portsmouth Harbour in the background will soon
change when the twin towers of the disused power station are demolished;
(*below*) Hythe Pier: standing out invitingly into Southampton Water the
pier provides a great flounder-catching platform for anglers who enjoy its
goodies for 12p a day

(*above*) Littlehampton: charter boats and fishing vessels packed tightly into the new marina where facilities for the angler are now excellent; (*below*) Brighton Marina: outside, the English Channel can be as rough as it likes; inside it's as calm as a millpond for the charter fleet

Black Bream

To the biologist, black bream and bass are in the same family order of fish (*percomorphi*) along with other bream, mackerel and mullet, and to the angler they are in the same category for fighting power. Bream are smaller than bass but on light tackle their darting, zig-zagging fight is a pleasure to experience. Once again the angler in the south enjoys all the best bream fishing in the country as they live mainly off the south coast. It is not surprising then that nearly half of all Britain's specimen black bream come from Dorset, Hampshire and Sussex. A 3lb fish is one of which to be proud.

Table 19

Specimen black bream in southern England

	1976	1975
Beach and boat combined	32%	41%
Boat caught	46%	56%
Beach caught	10%	20%

Bream live over rocks, rocky patches or rough broken ground feeding on small fish and sandeels. Best baits for bream are thin strips of squid or mackerel or ragworm, either drifted down on the tide on a long flowing trace on a running leger, or paternostered – provided the tackle is kept well on the move. Bream move through the south in a clearly discernible pattern. They first appear off Sussex as early as April, spreading slowly west into Hampshire during May. By June they are being taken in large numbers in both Sussex and Hampshire and by July they have begun to move westwards. By July and August – when they are being caught in strength in Dorset – they have mostly left Sussex save for a few stragglers.

Red Bream

These are taken mostly from deep water, over wrecks, and are rarer than black bream. In 1976 there was only one specimen red bream taken from the shore – from Portland Bill – and a quarter of all specimens in Britain came from the south. In 1975 eight red bream were taken from the shore, and four came from Dorset.

Grey Mullet

There are three species of grey mullet in Britain. The thick-lipped grey mullet is the most common, and is the fish most anglers refer to when they talk about mullet fishing. The others – thin-lipped grey mullet and golden grey mullet – are much rarer. The grey mullet is a powerful fish. Anglers need fine tackle to entice him to take a baited hook, and on such tackle this fish is a great fighter. A 2lb grey mullet is a beauty.

This species is grey and silvery, with six or seven horizontal lines along the body, the fins being white. Boat fishing in the south for grey mullet is the best in Britain, and nearly a quarter of all the country's specimens come from that area.

Table 20

Specimen grey mullet in southern England

	1976	1975
Beach and boat combined	23%	22%
Boat caught	66%	100%
Beach caught	20%	6%

Mullet live in harbours, estuaries and rivers, feeding on molluscs, algae and small larval creatures. Anglers have devised many baits, but favourites are flaked raw fish flesh (small pout for example), cheese, sausage meat and bread flake. Mullet fishing is as near freshwater fishing as the sea angler gets. Ground baiting is essential – implementing the useful advice of 'little and often', and float fishing is the most effective method.

Golden Grey Mullet

These are conspicuous by the golden spots on the gill cover. Very few are taken and of all seven caught in Britain in 1975 three came from Hampshire (all from Portsmouth Harbour), while in 1976 of the three specimens landed, two came from Hampshire. In 1980, Barry Mercer of the Portchester Sporting Angling Club set up a new British record with a 1lb 14oz fish from Portsmouth Harbour.

Incidentally, the red mullet are even rarer − yet again the angler in the south takes them to the exclusion of the rest of the country. In the 1975 season there were only four specimens landed in Britain − all from Dorset.

Conger Eel

Congers are powerful fish, known to have grown to more than 200lb in weight, and taken on rod and line above the much-revered 100lb mark. They live in rocks and wrecks and feed on any passing creature that gets near their razor-sharp teeth. The south has excellent conger grounds amid its rocky areas and just about half of all Britain's specimens in the mid 1970s came from this area.

Table 21

Specimen congers in southern England

	1976	1975
Beach and boat combined	45%	47%
Boat caught	50%	44%
Beach caught	33%	53%

Anglers chasing big congers need heavy tackle, with at least 12in of strong wire at the hook end of the trace to withstand the action of the conger's teeth. Fish baits are best − whole or half mackerel, herring, small live pout or squid. Once you have landed a conger do not place your hands near its mouth. The final wire sections of traces should be attached by means of snap-link swivels so that they can be undone − leaving the hook in the conger while you fish on. Your hooks can be retrieved later when the eels are good and dead.

Silver Eels

These made news in 1976 when it was decided that they were freshwater fish and were subject to the same fishing licence restrictions as trout and salmon. It was only the quick and persistent action of the NFSA which succeeded in reversing the decision which had meant a ban on all silver-eel fishing without a licence. The confusion had arisen because silver eels are both sea and freshwater fish. They are the green eels of freshwater venues, becoming silver eels (with silver bellies) as they begin migrating through estuaries and harbours. Exactly half of all the specimen silver eels in 1975 came from the south. No silver-eel specimen size has existed since the freshwater rumpus of 1976.

Turbot

These most-prized of all flatfish to the angler grow upwards of 20lb in weight and are fabulous to eat. They like a hard sandy ground and feed on fish, with sandeel as their favourite food. They are to be found wherever the tide is at its strongest.

The turbot is a round-shaped flatfish and has as its identifying feature small tubercles (bumps) all over its top sides. Its coloration is varied, mainly brown with white mottling, and it can adopt the colouring of its seabed surroundings. On average, a quarter of all specimen-sized turbot come from the south coast − with the added bonus in 1974 of all four specimen beach-caught turbot coming from the area.

Table 22

Specimen turbot in southern England

	1976	1975	1974
Beach and boat combined	28%	25%	36%
Boat caught	28%	25%	10%
Beach caught	−	−	100%

Brill

The only flatfish that could possibly be confused with the turbot is the brill. However, its identification features are quite distinct. The brill is more elongated and has no bumps at all, but the greatest difference is that the brill has scales and the turbot has not. The two species are often alike in colouring.

Brill, like the turbot, are found over hard sandy ground and feed on a similar diet, also liking to lie in a strong tide. May to September are the best months for taking brill. Although there are few specimens caught, about half those recorded have come from the south.

Table 23

Specimen brill in southern England

	1976	1975	1974
Beach and boat combined	43%	50%	17%
Boat caught	43%	60%	17%
Beach caught	—	—	—

As in the case of the turbot and the blonde ray the brill catches in the south have suffered with the recent deterioration of the Shambles Bank.

Mackerel

Nearly everyone who has fished in Britain in summer knows the mackerel; even the holiday-maker on mackerel charter boats can catch them in large numbers. This beautiful torpedo-shaped, strikingly marked green and black zig-zagged silver-bellied fish lives in shoals. On feathers it can be taken up to six-at-a-time and yet on very fine spinning gear from rocks and beaches where shoals swim in close, tremendous sport can be had from individual mackerel. Few anglers aim to catch big mackerel by design, but the south provides about a quarter of all the specimens taken. The greatest asset in catching mackerel is that they make the finest possible bait for many other species of fish. Their numbers have declined into the 1980s because of intensive commercial fishing in the west country.

Scad

Otherwise called the horse mackerel (a derogatory reference to the taste of its flesh), this fish is similar to the mackerel, although surprisingly it is not in the same biological family. It has large plate-like scales along its two lateral lines, having none of the mackerel's colouring, and it has much larger, bulging eyes. Anglers seldom go hunting for the scad, and they are usually taken by accident when mackerel spinning.

Among the remaining species taken in fewer numbers along the south coast are angler fish. Four specimen-sized monsters of this ugliest of all fish came from Chesil Beach out of a national beach-caught total of eight in 1975, yet not one specimen was seen anywhere in southern England in 1976.

In contrast, most of the little three-bearded rockling specimens in Britain come consistently from the south – 80 per cent of them in 1975.

The ling – most often associated with deep-water wrecks in the west country – are taken occasionally in the south, with about one tenth of all the nation's specimens coming from this area in 1976.

Other occasional surprises are taken, including John Dory, tub and red gurnard, garfish, sea trout and salmon.

3 Deep-Sea Fishing

Since the numbers of people flocking to sea to catch fish has increased, the chartering business along the south coast has become highly organised. Chartering is simply the carrying of anglers to marks where fish can be expected by skippers who hire out their boats and expert knowledge for a living. From the angler's point of view, chartering gives him an equal chance with the next man, of fishing the best marks along the south. He can rightfully expect that the skipper will put him where there is a good chance of fish, and can reasonably expect the skipper to be aided by all modern devices in achieving that aim. Once on the spot, the angler must then apply his own skill and experience in catching fish – and in a way the skipper should be able to expect him to do that adequately. For it is on the reputation of the catches aboard each charter boat that a business is built or lost. Of course, many charter skippers are happy to take out beginners and teach them from scratch, even to the extent of hiring out complete sets of tackle to the holiday-maker who has come 'on the spur of the moment' and is unprepared.

Along the southern coast of the English Channel, chartering caters for three main types of deep-water fishing – bottom fishing, wrecking, and sharking. The most common form of chartering is bottom fishing, varying throughout the area as the main species differ. In the winter months, for example, most boats will chase the cod and whiting. In summer, Littlehampton boats chase the black bream shoals. Many skippers have pet marks for skates and rays, and off Littlehampton and through the Nab area, packs of tope and spur-dog are hunted during the summer. Even if the skippers fail to hit the particular big fish they are after, most are careful to put their anglers over marks where some fish are feeding – so that failing all else, dogfish and

41

pout come aboard to keep the anglers happy. As an angler you can be pretty sure that a charter skipper is going to do his level best to put you where fish are expected – probably where he had a good day yesterday, or last week, or in the corresponding period of time last year. So, if you are not doing very well, before moaning about a useless skipper, ask yourself whether you are not to blame.

Fishing out of Langstone Harbour one day with all that harbour's top skippers on a special festival, I asked them what their pet hates were, and between them they gave me a picture of the charter skipper's greatest nightmare. He is the man who comes poorly clad (and then shivers and complains about the cold), who has inadequate tackle (and then loses his gear and has to borrow), who catches no fish (and moans that he wants to move) and then when the skipper moves he moans about the time spent travelling and lack of fishing time. He brings no food and drink (and moans because meals are not supplied) and finally takes no precautions against being sea-sick – though he knows he will be (and then wants to go in before he dies). Of course, there are no anglers who are all of these things, but it gives us a guide to how to ensure we are as proficient as possible before going chartering. Follow a few simple guidelines to ensure you will be a better angler, and you will likely benefit by catching more fish.

It is all a matter of good preparation. Always remember that it is colder at sea than ashore, and on days when you can get by ashore with one jumper, you will need two at sea. Apart from the very height of summer, you must allow for the weather to turn cold. Most charter trips last into the evening, when even warm days turn cool, and there is nothing more guaranteed to dampen spirits and turn anglers into unhappy and inefficient fishermen than an attack of the shivers. The secret of keeping warm and comfortable is to stay dry. Carry plenty of rags and cloth for wiping your hands. Wear or carry spare jumpers, and always take waterproof gear. If there is a sea running, even the best of charter boats will throw up spray. There are showers to catch the unwary, and an angler, once wet, quickly becomes uninterested in the day's fishing. For the same purpose, wellington boots or short rubber boots are a wise choice of footwear for charter trips. They serve the double purpose of keeping the feet dry – the first step to keeping them warm – and also they provide an efficient non-slip purchase on the boat's deck.

Turning up comfortably and warmly dressed is the right start. Make sure you are equipped with food and drink. A flask containing a hot beverage is a real tonic if you have been buffeted by a cold wind for several hours. Food will enable you to strengthen yourself on a long day – and surprisingly enough, will assist you in warding off the dreaded sea-sickness. It is worthwhile thinking about sea-sickness as it is the greatest single ruination of any day afloat. One person sick in a boat can affect others who are feeling queasy, and quickly start a chain reaction. If you know you suffer from sea-sickness, take anti-sick pills before the trip, and take dry food – bread or biscuits – which can help in settling your stomach. The English Channel is subject to some fairly long heavy rollers after a blow, and some strong tides which often react with winds to cause some boisterous movements among all sizes of boat.

And so to the tackle you should carry. First, before considering the details of the tackle, a stout tackle box is necessary. Plastic tackle boxes, compartmentalised for easy access, are best. They can expect to be covered in salt, rained on, overturned, knocked about and generally roughly handled – and they must stand up to such treatment. Salt instantly corrodes anything metal, so metal boxes should not be considered. Some anglers who are do-it-yourself enthusiasts build tackle boxes in wood which serve as seats, and which are fitted with strong straps so that the whole assembly can be thrown across the back and carried. Although a great deal of terminal tackle carried will depend on what species are being hunted, there is a basic supply of tackle which should stay in the tackle box for all trips.

It is necessary to carry weights in all shapes and forms. Some areas in southern England – south of the Isle of Wight, inside the West Solent, off the Needles, Beachy Head and around Portland Race – are renowned for fierce tides. I once fished the eastern seaboard of the Isle of Wight with 4lb of lead that eventually twisted and ruined a multiplier reel. For that end of the scale, weights around the 2lb mark need to be carried for the part of the day – in some cases just a few hours – when the tide is running full bore. As the tide slackens, an alert angler will constantly change his weights – provided they are present among his equipment. Always go armed with all sizes of weights, down to bombs of a few ounces.

What weights you will require depends entirely on what kind of line you use, and its breaking strain. Anglers have three choices – monofilament nylon, braided nylon like Dacron, or wire. Basically, the heavier breaking strain line you use, the thicker it will be; the thicker it is, the greater its resistance to the tide sweeping past it; and the greater the drag upon it, the heavier weight you will need to keep your tackle on the bottom.

It was to overcome the problem of having to use crippling weights in strong tides, that wire lines were developed and introduced around 1970. Tide-cutter single-strand wire – which is now virtually impossible to obtain – did exactly as its name implied. For the equivalent breaking strain of monofilament nylon, the wire was extremely thin, causing hardly any drag in the tide, and consequently pounds of lead could be exchanged for ounces of lead. That meant you could feel every movement on the seabed, instead of suffering the insensitive blur that nylon line users experienced in heavy tides. It had disadvantages like kinking and snapping easily, and with coils tending to spring off the reel. In the 'wire revolution' which came during the early 1970s most anglers from charter boats – especially off Hampshire (Needles, Dunnose, Nab) or Portland Race, where tides race hardest – tried wire. Many were instantly sold on it, learned to beat its disadvantages and stayed with it. Others found it expensive stuff to lose to breakages and went back to their trusty old nylon – heavy weights and all. The arguments for and against wire are often debated and it is a personal choice, but anglers who have stuck with wire, mastered its use in areas where tides run hard, score better results on average when chasing the bigger species like conger, bull huss, skates and rays.

Kitting yourself out with wire gear is expensive and there is no way around it. You need a rod with metal roller rings throughout its length and a double roller at the tip. You need a large-diameter metal-spooled multiplier reel, and the wire itself is very expensive. There are two main types on the market – single-strand stainless wire which is the most expensive – or seven-strand, twisted stainless wire, which although slightly less expensive, is still dear. The twisted wire is thinner for its equivalent breaking strain and therefore slightly more effective in its prime aim at enabling you to fish with less lead, but there is the problem of individual strands breaking. There is no stretch in wire, and you are therefore in direct contact with the terminal tackle − and biting fish. But it is advisable to give yourself a buffer to absorb the shock of striking. Most anglers do this by means of a leader of strong nylon − often doubled − about 15ft long between the end of the wire and the terminal tackle. The leader also means that when you have reeled in to rebait or unhook fish, the nylon − and not the wire − is being manhandled and exposed to rubbing when you put your rod down.

Back to the tackle box. If you include a selection of swivels, booms, links and hooks, you will always be in a position to adapt to changes encountered afloat. You may go afloat aiming at one species of fish with one set of tackle in mind but with the basic ingredients in your tackle box, you can always adapt. With such a large variety of fishing encountered in the south, it is advisable to carry spools of different breaking strain line. There are many bream trips which produce conger for the angler who can find a wire trace in his box, and many cod can be taken by the man who, after catching whiting, can change up to a heavier trace by having some instantly available. The greatest asset of any tackle is to have it so organised in your box that you know just where any item is − and can reach it. It sounds so simple to say that the man who catches most fish is the one whose line is in the water longest, but many people ignore this fact. If you get broken up and can find a complete change of terminal tackle in a few seconds you will be fishing again in moments. If your tackle box is lacking in items, or is in one enormous tangle − and some tangles have to be seen to be believed − then it could take up to ten minutes to get down again. Repeat that a few times during the day and you will have lost more than half-an-hour's fishing time. To avoid this situation, one solution is to make up a selection of traces for your box before a projected trip. Maybe a few wire traces in case you connect with congers. Have several bream traces available when chasing this species, to beat breakages on the rocky ground beneath the bream. It always pays to be prepared for the unexpected. In summer months always have a set of mackerel feathers set up in your box. Throughout the English Channel, mackerel run in heavy shoals during the summer – and at any time a skipper may drop you over a shoal. If you can instantly get to your feathers and drop them over you will be ahead of the angler fumbling through his tangled box to unthread his string while you are catching fish. As like as not, by the time he unravels his puzzle, the shoal could have passed by. Similarly, keep a set of light flatfish gear in the box – spoons, beads, light traces, fine hooks. They take up little space and can make a day if dabs or plaice suddenly come on the feed. In 1976 a winter cod trip out of Rye brought in no cod, but 144 dabs instead – thanks to the anglers aboard having the necessary tackle to adapt when the first dabs went on the feed.

The two major items of tackle you need afloat are the rod and reel, and once again the right choice beforehand makes a day a success or a failure. For most charter trips out of southern ports, where big fish can reasonably be expected and where strong tides can be encountered, multipliers reels are favourite, or centre-pins or, possibly, heavy fixed-spool reels. Small fixed-spool reels are seldom man enough for the task, and in general they are frowned on aboard charter boats. With casting never required, the main fear that beginners have with multipliers – that of 'bird-nests' – is removed, and they can be used confidently for the type of fishing their designers had in mind. Even quite a small skate or huss can put a tough strain on a reel when you are heaving them against a boring tide. The rod is also a vital factor in the landing of big fish. Most boat rods are between 6ft and 8ft long, and many anglers fishing charter boats find general-purpose boat rods perfectly adequate. They will handle most fish encountered – rays and small congers – without being over-powerful, and also smaller fish like the pout or dogfish. Rods that are frowned upon on charter trips are those over 10ft long, being unwieldy and getting in everyone's way, and also short billiard-cue types which allow the angler to enjoy hardly any sport, and which do nothing to help him detect bites or feel fish.

After following the foregoing guidelines the angler is basically ready for his trip. A few added refinements – like the carrying of a knife, a torch for winter trips, pliers if he is expecting to use wire gear, and a supply of polythene bags to put his fish in – and the angler will not only show himself as a competent useful chap, but he should find that his catches improve.

So much for preparing for the charter trip. Next we can look at what the angler can expect to find among the charter-boat fleets in the south. When making bookings, be sure the boat you choose is registered and licensed. To be registered it must comply with stringent regulations governing its sea-worthiness, the safety equipment it carries, its range and permitted fishing areas, and its skipper must be a proficient seaman. If you were to take a model charter boat you could reasonably expect it to have a covered wheelhouse area large enough to shelter the whole party, facilities possibly for a brew-up, some seating arrangements round the gunwales, and toilets. Most charter boats along the south coast are equipped with echo-sounders and you can reasonably expect your skipper to have one to help him precisely locate fishing marks. Most have radios among their safety equipment – an item of vital importance. On one trip when we were unable to return from near the Nab Tower, we were able to radio ashore to inform relatives not to worry, and while the skipper successfully repaired the engine, we caught two more cod – including a fish of 24lb. Steaming time to and from deep-water marks is another factor, and experience alone can tell you whether a boat is fast or slow. There are few south-coast marks that are less than an hour's steaming from the main ports, and much of the best fishing comes after two or more hours' steaming.

About the only exception is for wrecking when the steaming times can be longer for the deeper wrecks. But most aspects of wrecking charters are a little more specialised than ordinary charters. The angler needs to be slightly more prepared, and the boats need to be somewhat better equipped. The angler will be afloat longer, travel further, need to be even better protected against the weather, definitely have waterproof gear and be capable of feeding and watering himself for a longer period. His tackle also needs to be more carefully prepared. If the charter hits the chosen wreck on good form, the angler can expect to lose plenty of gear. At worst he will lose terminal tackle by snagging the wreck and at best he will lose tackle to being smashed up by big fish – probably congers. Many of the wrecks in the Channel off central southern England are set in heavy tidal areas, so the angler will need heavier weights than those used for a normal charter. Wire traces are essential when wrecking for congers, and it pays to have plenty of made-up traces available in order to save time. One additional item that is important is a butt-pad as it can become hard work reeling up heavy congers regularly from a good wreck if you are unable to gain a good purchase for the rod butt. Additional terminal tackle solely for wrecking consists mainly of pirks and artificial lures, such as red-gills or large feathers.

When considering which charter boat to aim for for wrecking facilities, the main additional equipment you would expect would be Decca navigation gear. This is expensive equipment hired by skippers which enables them to sail to a precise spot on a gridded map. By learning for themselves the exact positions of wrecks, they can sail to known points over such wrecks. The echo-sounder then enables them to locate the wreck on the seabed, and either drift over it or anchor uptide.

Sharking is an altogether more specialised form of chartering, and is really confined to the waters off the back of the Isle of Wight, and to boats out of Portsmouth, Langstone, Lymington and the Island itself – Yarmouth or Bembridge. Central southern England is not as popular as the west country for sharking, although during the late 1960s and early 1970s some of the results from south of the Isle of Wight were as good as the west country catches. In nearly all cases, the angler chartering a shark boat hires the entire equipment, and is not expected to bring his own. Charter boats lay on powerful rods together with heavy multiplier reels loaded with heavy line, and terminal tackle, and the skipper usually baits up himself. With many of the favoured shark drifts during the summer being made from the area south of St Catherine's Point either east towards Ventnor or west towards the Needles, the steaming time before reaching the shark grounds is always longer than for most trips – sometimes over three hours. The triple advantage of sharking trips is that while the angler on the shark lines awaits action, two other kinds of fishing can carry on – mackerel feathering and bottom drifting. Shark fishing is always carried out during summer months when the mackerel are in, and south of the Isle of Wight heavy mackerel shoals build up. While enjoying sport with mackerel, you are also supplying fresh bait for the shark lines and extra raw material for the rubby-dubby supplies. At the same time you can choose to drift the seabed, where pollack are often taken and even tope packs are encountered. Even if shark fail to show on shark trips, it is not often that you fail to find any sport.

As with all kinds of chartering, the skipper is a vital link in the success or failure of any trip. The angler needs to pick a skipper who is worth his salt. A good skipper is one whose boat is totally equipped – and there are many boats which fall far short of good standards. He is a skipper with a good selection of marks at his fingertips so that weather and tide variations can be countered and even used to advantage. He should be around during the trip to assist with fishing. There are very good skippers who help sort out tangled lines, who help unhook and dispatch fish, and who take time to assist beginners. There are bad skippers who drop anchor and go below for a sleep, leaving the customers to their own devices. A good skipper will try different marks if several hours of fishing have drawn a blank and he can see no advantage of tide coming his way. So the problem for the angler is how to find out who are the good skippers and who are the bad. One way is to visit local tackle shops in the port from which you are fishing. Most of them carry advertisements for charter skippers. Tackle dealers learn from experience which anglers return after trips on which boats. Their opinion is often a safe pointer towards good skippers and good boats.

Finally, the angler chartering a boat should remember his responsibility to the rest of the party. This begins from the time you set out on a trip. Always be on time, and if for some reason you are unable to put in an appearance, ring to let the boatman or the party organiser know. There is nothing more infuriating than for a party to have to sit waiting for one late angler.

The way you conduct yourself throughout a trip can help or hinder the rest of the party. Anglers sitting towards the bows of anchored boats – uptide – need heavy leads to prevent their lines drifting aft and tangling. Anglers sitting towards the stern – downtide – should fish with slightly lighter leads so that their lines run well aft away from the boat. With simple common sense a party of twelve can fish without infuriating tangles. It takes only one angler acting irresponsibly to disturb a whole trip. When someone hooks a big fish, it is helpful for those immediately near him to reel their lines up out of the way. If you should hook a big fish, you would hope that your colleagues would do the same for you, so that the fish cannot tangle round their lines. Take precautions against sea-sickness; your being sick could spoil other anglers' fun. Remember that in contributing to the trip by behaving responsibly, you will also increase your chances of catching fish.

This form of sea work gives the angler the best chance of catching the bigger species and the south's charter boats' activities are as follows. The boats chasing mixed fishing provide skate and rays (mainly three species), the dogfish family (spur-dog, bull huss, lesser spotted dogfish and smoothhounds) and tope. In the summer, charter boats aim especially at black bream, and in the winter they aim particularly at cod.

Wreck charter boats aim at catching congers, and pollack in the south. Wreck boats also catch black bream. Red bream and ling – common on wrecks in the west country – are rarer from the south's wrecks.

The shark charter boats mainly aim to catch porbeagles in the south, although in 1976 the Isle of Wight grounds yielded more threshers than porbeagles. Blue sharks – which are the commonest in the west country – are less numerous than porbeagles in the south.

In addition to the fish which charter boats particularly set out to catch, they often hit a variety of extra species. These include turbot and brill, monkfish and angler fish.

(*above*) Hastings Pier: fishing from the lower platform gives anglers the best sport. Here Hastings front is spread out to the east; (*below*) Beachy Head, Sussex: off these clifflands are the famous bass and tope areas – firm favourites with many Sussex anglers

(*above*) Newhaven East Pier, Sussex: this is the easternmost of Newhaven's two breakwater piers, and it attracts anglers throughout the year; (*below*) Portchester Creek: at the end of the day the sun goes down across the mudflats of Portchester Creek where the Roman castle stands sentinel over the upper reaches of Portsmouth Harbour

4 Chartering in Dorset

Chartering in Dorset is centred on the two major ports of Weymouth and Poole, with a few boats chartering from lesser ports on a small scale. Mention the word Weymouth, and anglers will have two pictures flash into their minds like beacons – the Shambles (with its turbot and rays) and Portland Bill (with the bass in the Race). Talk about Poole, and anglers will tell you about the bass in its entrance, the black bream off the Old Harry Rocks, and mixed fishing all over Poole Bay.

Weymouth's chartering business is going through a time of change, forced on it by the environment at sea and the fish catches of recent years. Boats working out of Weymouth are having to seek new horizons since the Shambles fishing has slowed down, and since bass catches have decreased from Portland Race. Some boats are being equipped with Decca navigational equipment and are searching out the wrecks in the Channel, and some are now even offering sharking trips. The Shambles Bank lies about nine miles out from Weymouth to the west of Portland Bill and consists of sand, shingle and shells. Its composition attracts small fish, especially sandeels (and they in turn attract the big fish), flatties, bass, pollack, and even tope together with great numbers of rays. But the great days of the Shambles, when trips would virtually guarantee that several huge turbot were caught, are over. Some people blame trawlers for stripping the bank of its fish, and others blame the great quantities of pollution that man pours into the sea every day. Maybe the answer is that a combination, plus other factors, have decreased the fish population. But if the biggest fish have gone, there is still a good variety left to be caught – especially from the west end of the bank. Thornbacks, small-eyed rays, pollack, bass, plaice, dabs and an occasional turbot or blonde ray will provide an angler with a pleasing and enjoyable day. It is still necessary to go equipped with fairly heavy tackle as you could encounter a good fish.

More often than not, the charter boats now travel beyond the Shambles to new marks in deeper water − rocky patches further out that are beginning to yield good conger, for example. For this angling the enthusiast needs to be prepared for really heavy going as the tides out there are strong, and you can expect to be taking big conger out of rough rock.

Weymouth's other unique attraction − especially for the mid-summer to autumn charterer − is the bass fishing in Portland Race. In the whole of the southern central England coastline there is no fiercer tide race than that off Portland, with its roaring seas and overfalls boiling in confusion. It is not surprising. The tide ripping down both sides of Portland Bill meet off the Bill itself where they also clash with the main stream tide in the English Channel. On top of this, the area is rich in craggy rock-points jutting up into this maelstrom of water. Here, it is a case of tremendous fishing when you can get it. The Race which provides the conditions that the bass love also produces impossible fishing conditions − with unmanageable confused seas and raging foam. But on a day when the weather is kind and the tide is right the Race becomes a bass fisherman's paradise, with the tide helping to activate the red-gill's movements and the bass snapping at anything. Fishing Portland Race is not to be done with any old tackle. Many charter boats provide the tackle − and it has to be strong. Line up to 30lb breaking strain is often used, and the secret is to use a long flowing trace with the red-gills. Some experimentation is possible with lures, and small pirks and mackerel strips will take bass here. The Race is treacherous, so great care is always needed. Occasionally pollack are taken and quite often the bass caught here are double-figure fish.

Weymouth has a third wealth of fishing which can be reached at most times. This is the mixed fishing in grounds across Weymouth Bay into Ringstead Bay and even as far east as Lulworth Rocks. All the best fishing marks are over patches of rock in the offshore limits of Weymouth Bay. Conger are taken from the rocks, with pout all the year through, bream predominantly in late summer, and pollack and bass. On one such trip over a mark well out in Weymouth Bay we had an angler connect with a cheeky porbeagle. On medium-heavy gear the angler guided one of the shark's runs alongside the boat. It motored to a standstill directly beneath the gunwale – but far too deep for a gaff to reach. He stayed there long enough for us all to admire him before accelerating away from the boat and going for another circuit of his domain in Weymouth Bay. Once more he returned to upset the excited angler before changing direction and moving away under the keel – snapping the line on his way through.

Sharks are not the only big fish you might bump into in Weymouth Bay, for big rays are occasionally caught. Mackerel shoals and the packs of tope that feed on them are both encountered, and dogfish and whiting fill into the Bay marks in winter. The opportunity of finding rough-ground marks in Weymouth-based boats extends as far as Lulworth Rocks which lie about two miles west of Lulworth. Conger are found in these rocks together with all the mixed species usually expected over rough ground. Be prepared to meet some big fish here.

East of Weymouth there are no major chartering ports until you reach Poole – which is a kind of Mecca for anglers who cannot afford the time or travelling expense to reach the west country chartering but who want good access, plenty of boats, and a fine variety of fishing to occupy them all year. Poole has the largest chartering fleet anywhere in Dorset, Hampshire or Sussex with between 30 and 40 boats available. Many of them can be booked through an agency which handles the administration for about half of them, while other skippers prefer to function independently and they can be booked privately.

Outside Poole Harbour good fishing potential extends for about 12 miles in either direction – right to Christchurch Ledge in the east and to St Alban's Head and beyond, in exceptional circumstances, to the south and west. Passing out of the harbour the angler is moving through some of the best fishing grounds of all – the bass runs in the entrance. Anglers who net sandeels off Sandbanks and drift-line the entrance usually enjoy the best sport.

Immediately south of the entrance, across Studland Bay, is the famous headland with the Old Harry Rocks at its foot. Many years ago there was an 'Old Harry's Wife' as well as 'Old Harry'

– but years ago the 'wife' disappeared into the sea and 'Old Harry' himself is being eroded. South of the rocks there are a number of headlands running down to the Purbeck Peninsula, each with a ledge where fishing is worthwhile. These are Ballard Point, Peveril Point and Anvil Point, round Durlston Head facing south and finally St Alban's Head round the peninsula.

Fishing these southern most headlands is dependent on the weather, and with a strong south-westerly or southerly blowing, the boats will not venture that far south where strong tides combine to bring some hectic conditions. But on days like this the true depth of Poole's potential comes into play. For then, there are the mass of marks to the east. Immediately east out of Poole Harbour are the Poole Patch rocks – the Inner Patch, the Westmuth Rocks and the Outer Poole Patch. Further across Poole Bay to the east is the Southbourne Rough about three miles south of Southbourne – and even further east is Christchurch Ledge still within range of the Poole boats. Further south and across the furthest extent of Poole Bay are areas of reefs and rocks which produce the big species.

With that wealth of fishing Poole offers something to the charter angler all through the year. The season begins in April and May when the earliest black bream come in – a species for which the Old Harry Rocks are famous. They are taken further south, down to Durlston Head – and weather permitting, even round the corner to the Dancing Ledges off Seacombe Cliff and Anvil Point. These more southerly marks give the added chance of pout, pollack, dogfish, conger and rays. Most of the charter boats are out in force from mid-May to June when the bream are in full cry from the Old Harry Rocks south to Ballard Point. Sometimes boats fish right under the clifflands in 40ft of water. You can expect to lose some tackle on these trips in the rocks and it pays to have a few long traces ready made up so that no time is lost when a new set of tackle is needed.

The variety of species taken along with the bream during the summer is terrific. On one breaming trip out of Poole we caught bream, red gurnard, pout, dogfish, and a small cuckoo wrasse in that order so that only one of the first five fish on board was a bream. In the summer charter boats will move across to the Outer Poole Patch, occasionally just inside to the Westmuth Rocks, and less often to the Inner Patch. Bream, pollack, bass and small conger are taken on these trips. But in mid-summer, if the weather is ideal the charter skippers prefer to steam for two hours south-south-east to the offshore reefs where some good fish are brought up – including congers to 40lb, tope, more bream and pollack. On a day of absolutely perfect weather the boats will venture round into Kimmeridge Bay for some really excellent fishing. Skippers will only make the trip if the forecast too is perfect – so such trips are few and far between. But once there the conger fishing, big ray and big bass hunting is first class. Later in the summer the reef marks offshore fish better and better with pollack up to 10lb among the still lingering bass, and with tope lasting through June and July and occasionally into August.

In autumn all the marks are still producing their mixed bags and from October onwards Poole swings into its winter routine – which again means variety and choice for the angler. The Old Harry Rocks – or the area a little way off – produce whiting and cod. Southbourne Rough is visited by the charter boats seeking cod (with whiting, pout and dogfish filling the waiting gaps). The same species together with small congers and pollack are taken from the Outer Poole Patch when the weather sometimes forces the big charter boats to abandon the deeper offshore marks. Skippers travelling south to Peveril Point hope to contact pollack, conger and some cod, but as the winter weather worsens few boat skippers will contemplate the risk of rounding Durlston Head. Once the winter begins to fade in February, the area has its only quiet time when the February and March doldrums overtake the sport. During most of the year – except winter – the night fishing from Poole is as productive as day fishing, and conger enthusiasts swear that it is better.

Chartering is carried on on a far smaller scale from two other ports in Dorset – West Bay at Bridport in the west and Christchurch on the border with Hampshire in the east.

Chartering from West Bay is restricted by two major factors – weather conditions which are often adverse, and the difficulties of negotiating the harbour entrance when the wind is blowing from the south or south-west. Bridport itself is two miles inland but the harbour at West Bay is protected by a narrow channel between two sea walls with two stone piers at the entrance to the sea. At low tide the entrance almost dries out and is of no use to boats, and whenever the wind blows onshore a difficult sea builds up inside the channel to the harbour, often making it quite impossible to navigate. Trips out of West Bay are usually aimed at the rock patches about four miles offshore in Lyme Bay where black bream is a summer quarry, but where conger, pollack, wrasse, pout and dogfish can also be expected. In the winter and especially after Christmas when the worst weather prevails, the fishing drops off dramatically.

Some chartering takes place at Christchurch, with the Southbourne Rough grounds accessible to the west once the boats round Hengistbury Head. Christchurch Ledge is an obvious target with a few rough patches available in Christchurch Bay. Some boats travel south and pick up the very eastern end of the offshore reefs stretching south of Poole Bay and Hengistbury. Christchurch Ledge − which runs out for nearly three miles from Hengistbury Head − is most usually fished from the Poole side where a good variety of small fish (pollack, pout, bream and dogfish) are regular feeders. An occasional huss, conger or tope is taken, but some of the area's best tope marks are around the Christchurch Ledge buoy at the outer end of the ledge.

5 Chartering in Hampshire: The Needles and the Nab

The waters from the Needles at the westernmost tip of the Isle of Wight to Selsey Bill – including the Solent, the Needles grounds, the Nab Tower grounds and Spithead – are among the most heavily chartered areas along the south coast, the main fleets being centred on Langstone Harbour, Chichester Harbour and Bembridge (to the east), and Lymington, Keyhaven and Yarmouth, Isle of Wight (in the west).

The Needles marks provide probably the best deep-water fishing in the whole area, a reputation based on huge catches in the past – including probably the only spot in Hampshire where skate over 100lb were caught. It is some years now since the area produced a big skate, and many of the Island anglers who used to fish for them out of Yarmouth reckon they are gone for good – their natural habitat ruined by the dredgers operating in the area of the Pot Bank. The best of the skate reported from the Bank scaled 130lb. The Pot Bank used to lie about 1½ miles south-west of the Needles. During the 1970s dredgers began working on it, taking away its sand and gravel until the entire bank was removed. When the marine authorities finally removed the Pot Bank buoy, one of the most famous marks in the Needles repertoire had disappeared forever – taking with it the best big skate fishing along the south coast. When anglers knew they might encounter a 'ton up' skate they used to go prepared. Nowadays, few anglers are kitted out to hold big skate and the occasional monster that is contacted is usually lost. In the late 1970s at least two big skate were hooked and one estimated at 90lb was lost at the gunwale.

But there are many other big specimens that attract the Yarmouth, Lymington and Keyhaven charter fleets to the Needles grounds. The Needles cod in winter run to over 40lb

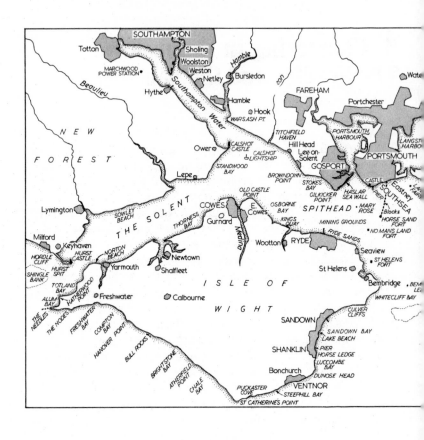

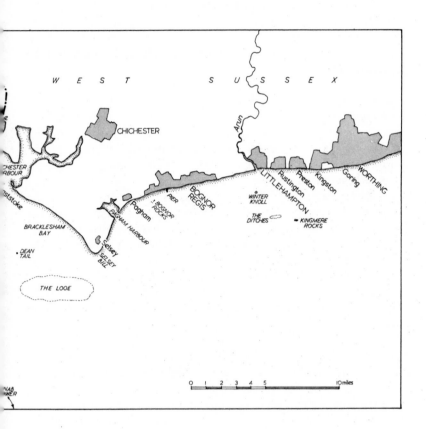

WEST SUSSEX

CHICHESTER

Arun

CHICHESTER
HARBOUR

stoke

BRACKLESHAM
BAY

• DEAN
TAIL

THE LOOE

Pagham

PAGHAM HARBOUR

Selsey

SELSEY
BILL

BOGNOR
ROCKS

PIER

BOGNOR
REGIS

WINTER
KNOLL

THE
DITCHES

KINGMERE
ROCKS

LITTLEHAMPTON

Rustington

Preston

Kingston

Goring

WORTHING

NAB
OWER

0 1 2 3 4 5   10 miles

with the 1979 season being a bonanza. Tope not only come in great packs but they run to 50lb in size, and even the pout and whiting run big − whiting to nearly 4lb and pout almost to 3lb. All fishing off the Needles area is subject to strong tides, which have a direct bearing on fishing methods and which can be turned to the angler's benefit.

Very heavy tackle will usually be needed for chartering in this area. Frequently 2lb or 3lb of lead can be needed, and wire line and wire traces are often used. It is sensible to use traces at least 6ft in length, allowing the baits to work in the tide. Favourite baits on charter trips are whole, sides or lasks of mackerel for tope, skate, huss and conger, while the cod fishing in winter is something on its own.

Cod catches around the Needles marks were at their best in the 1960s when boats took catches of up to ten at a time. During the early 1970s they dwindled but there was a welcome revival towards the 1980s and skippers in 1980 were comparing the season with those good old days of the sixties. Big cod have made up the bulk of these catches, including many of 35lb and mostly all above the 20lb mark. Hundreds of excellent cod were taken, crowned by some memorable beauties which topped the 40lb mark.

Two of the best baits for cod in this area are squid and whole live pout. One favourite method is to use the slack tide period to catch yourself some small pout on light gear and then use the pout for bait as the tide picks up. Anyone who has caught a large cod will remember its cavernous mouth and for that reason the necessity of using big baits will be obvious. When using squid, the favourite trick is to use the North American Calimari squid whole − or even with two on a hook together. In the Needles area great packs of dogfish make themselves a nuisance by attacking the big baits put down for cod. Squid has one advantage over fish baits in that it is tougher and usually remains on the hook despite the attention of dogfish, which usually succeed only in stripping off the head and tentacles.

During the winter months conger catches go hand in hand with the cod in the Needles area. For congers − which will take squid intended for cod − mackerel is a better bait. It is because congers are likely to be caught that wire traces are used to give you some chance against the eel's razor-like teeth. Some anglers do not like using wire traces, arguing that the wire prohibits the bait from flowing naturally in the tide. The best way to overcome the problem is to use a heavy nylon trace, with a short wire section attached by swivel at the hook end of the trace.

One of the finest tope fishing grounds in the south is in the tide race between the Needles and the Shingles Bank, an area noted for its large mackerel concentrations – a natural feeding draw for the tope. Fresh mackerel, preferably caught as you fish, is the top bait and many cuts can be used. The added attraction of catching mackerel as you fish is that they can be used as the raw material for the rubby-dubby bag. Like their larger brethren, the sharks, the tope will be attracted by rubby-dubby, and keeping a stream of freshly mashed and bloodied mackerel drifting into the tide will keep tope interested. When using mackerel, a fillet, a belly section, head and guts or tail slice will attract tope, and with a smaller bait there is a better chance of the hook striking home.

In the autumn and winter season of 1976 an exciting new phenomenom occurred both in the Needles and Nab areas – the sudden arrival of good-sized pollack where they had not been known before, in large numbers. Happily the trend is still going strong into the eighties. In the Needles area pollack were not taken to any good size before 1970 and the Island record stood at about 3lb for a long while. In the mid 1970s a stir was created when the record suddenly rocketed to about 7lb – and there it stood. In 1976 boats all round the Island began taking pollack when the anglers were bottom fishing for congers, huss and skate. In the Needles ground more than a dozen came up over the 10lb mark, and the new record went to a fish over 16lb. These catches fell to anglers not particularly hunting for pollack, and although it is premature to see any firm trend in the catches of a few years, it does seem that the pollack have become regular feeders round the Island waters. Several eminent anglers have put forward theories ranging from the increase in water temperature after the summer drought of 1976, to it being the fault of the Russians killing off huge quantities of the mackerel shoals further west, and forcing fish eastwards to find alternative food supplies.

Yarmouth skippers extend their sphere of operations round the Needles into Freshwater Bay when they are after conger, which are taken in rocky areas. Sometimes they will travel as far east as Brook Ledge for the pleasure. If extremely bad weather prevents skippers from getting to the Needles grounds they will sometimes fish in the West Solent – choosing the Solent banks off Newtown where tope run, or Hamstead Ledge where they will expect to catch bass or spotted rays. This mainly applies from June to September. One new trend which is pleasing to skippers is a growing run of black bream between the northern edge of the Shingles Bank and Hurst Spit.

About 25 miles to the east are the main offshore fishing grounds for the charter fleets out of the mainland ports of Langstone Harbour, and to a lesser degree from Portsmouth and Chichester Harbours. Charter boats out of Bembridge also fish these waters. Their focal point is the Nab Tower which stands about nine miles south of Langstone Harbour in the English Channel and 4½ miles east of the Island. For ten months of the year these grounds produce good general fishing, with at least three species of ray, bull huss, conger, dogfish and pout being caught all the time, and packs of spur-dog, smoothhound and tope chasing the mackerel into the waters during the summer, and with whiting and renowned cod fishing during the winter. February and March are about the only two quiet months – a time when most charter-boat owners choose to take their craft out of the water for the annual overhaul and refit.

Langstone Harbour has the biggest charter fleet of any of the mainland harbours in Hampshire with fully prepared boats running regular day and night trips, weekdays and weekends. They operate from two pick-up points, the ferry pontoon on the Hayling side of Langstone Harbour (near its mouth) and at the ferry pontoon on the Portsmouth side (which is less often used). Only a couple of charter boats run out of Portsmouth Harbour.

Chichester Harbour also has a far smaller charter business, the boats operating from Emsworth Quay in the upper reaches of the harbour. They have a half-hour steam across the harbour before reaching the entrance and before steaming out to their offshore grounds which include Bracklesham Bay towards Selsey Bill as well as the Nab and Spithead grounds.

Mostly these charter fleets provide mixed bottom fishing, but a few boats equipped with Decca navigational aids run wreck trips beyond the Nab Tower, and in recent years they have begun catering for shark enthusiasts.

Most favoured grounds are those around the Nab Tower. Several miles south of the Nab Tower are the Spoil Grounds – a huge natural hole in the seabed which has been a dumping ground for spoil from dredgers for decades – a first-class area for mixed fishing, especially congers, rays and spur-dogs. After dropping off in the mid 1970s, the spur-dog packs have now returned and are appearing in the same large numbers as before. Three main species of ray come from the Nab grounds – mainly the thornbacks, but with plenty of small-eyed rays and slightly fewer spotted rays. Other rays are caught occasionally, and when they come in, they are usually good fish. There was that British record eagle ray, and in my column I reported two sting rays over 30lb in one day in 1976, and blonde rays to 25lb.

To the east of the Nab, charter boats frequent a patch of rough ground to the south and south-east of Bullocks Patch. The Bullocks Patch buoy itself is about six miles south of Chichester Harbour, and is in the range of private boats. Fishing there ten years ago was excellent with small boats catching conger, rays, huss, pout and dogfish. Nowadays the Patch fishes more slowly – except for the black bream fishing which remains first class in summer.

Inside the Nab Tower there are numerous marks which are fished all the year round. These include New Grounds – a large bank which has the Nab Rock at its centre. Nab Rock is a favoured cod mark, producing well in 1979, and it also has a good reputation for bream in the summer. A deep gulley lies to the south of the Nab East buoy which produces good mixed fishing, while further inside the Nab – well within the reach of smaller boats – are the Dean Tail, Dean Elbow, and 25-minute mark locations, used universally and dealt with in Chapter 12. One happy feature about all these marks is that the cod they produce are usually big fish towards the 20lb size.

To the east the charter boats from Langstone and Chichester fish as far as Selsey Bill. There are marks in Bracklesham Bay to the south of the 'targets' – wreck-marking poles which provide good mixed fishing and which are visited especially for the whiting in winter. The two main marks fished off Selsey Bill are the Boulder Bank spots (about 2½ miles south) and in the Looe

Channel (a channel about 1½ miles south of the Bill which runs through the rocks). A favourite chartering spot is a deep hole south of the Boulder Bank which produces the big specimens of rays, congers and cod. Boulder Bank is also a top bream mark in summer.

To the west of a centre line from Langstone Harbour to the Nab Tower are the grounds close to the eastern seaboard of the Isle of Wight. Favourite of these is Dunnose Head, which is a prolific mark for some of the few Portsmouth boats. Tides are notoriously strong through this wildly rocky area, and anglers should only fish with wire. Sometimes, neap tides give the only comfortable chance of fishing the area, but results – especially with conger eels – can be spectacular. Bull huss are regularly taken over 10lb from the same area and the spur-dog packs that usually frequent the Nab area are also found at Dunnose.

The remainder of the eastern coastline of the Island – Sandown Bay, Culver Cliffs, the Princessa Shoal off the eastern foreland up to Bembridge Ledge – provides fishing grounds for charter boats sheltering from bad weather. The position of the Island and the shelter it affords is another benefit to the charter fleets from these Hampshire harbours. When the predominant south-westerly blows and puts the Nab grounds and marks further east into an uncomfortably rough zone, there are marks inside the eastern Solent which provide fishing and shelter. When the wind swings to the west and blows hard, Culver Cliffs provide the same two features. Among the favourite sheltered marks for charter boats are the Mining Grounds in the Solent off Ryde which produce good skate fishing (I once pulled up a 17lb thornback there, belonging to another angler who had let it swim round my line) and some of the other banks inside the Solent, like the Ryde Middle. Boat marks off Culver Cliffs have produced cod over 20lb and Sandown Bay some big congers from its rocky patches, including one by Roy Atkins of 53lb.

Shark fishing in the waters south of the Isle of Wight went through a slack period in the mid 1970s, but improved again towards the eighties. The late 1960s and early 1970s established the grounds with several former porbeagle British records being smashed by Island sharks. The main shark waters are the deep-water drifts off St Catherine's Point – either to the west towards the Needles or to the east towards Ventnor and the Nab Tower.

Shark charters are run from Yarmouth and Bembridge on the Island, and Chichester, Langstone and Lymington on the mainland. Porbeagle sharks form the bulk of the catches but with a surprising trend towards more threshers in the late 1970s. Makos have occasionally been reported sighted. One of the recognised authorities on sharking in Britain, Trevor Housby, writing about the Isle of Wight grounds in the early 1970s described them as the 'top porbeagle hot spot' at that time.

The thresher revolution has been a really exciting boost to the area's fishing. The thresher with its distinctive tail, is far more powerful and more spectacular a fighter than the porbeagle but comparatively few are caught on rod and line in this country. It was a particularly memorable July day in the mid 1970s when I had phone calls from two skippers reporting that they had both landed a thresher within hours of each other in the grounds south of the Nab Tower. The bigger thresher – at 262lb – had been landed aboard the Portsmouth Harbour boat *Shark Hunter V* (skippered by Dave Speller) and had fought against its captor, Peter Higgins, for three hours and three minutes. It came from the Ventnor end of the usual drifting area. At the other end, off St Catherine's Point, another thresher of 192lb was landed aboard the Langstone Harbour boat, *Langstone Jaffa* (skippered by Bob White). Its captor, teenager Peter Knight, had done battle for 55 minutes. Within two weeks another Langstone skipper, Colin Smith, rang me to report the capture of a third thresher, weighing 76lb, which he had beaten personally on tope gear aboard his boat *Salacia*. The Shark Angling Club of Great Britain gave its top award for the best shark of the year to Peter Higgins' big thresher together with the award for the best thresher. That one was the biggest thresher in British waters at that time for 18 years and the fourth biggest of *all* time. But even that fish was bettered when the new British record thresher, a fabulous giant weighing 295lb, was taken by H. Jim Aris off Dunnose Head in 1978.

The decline in the porbeagle catches in the mid 1970s brought forth several theories about where they had gone. The activity of the Russian fishermen in the west country wiping out the mackerel has been widely believed to be the culprit. The theory goes that because there are fewer mackerel surviving in the west country, there are fewer reaching the waters off the Island.

Consequently there are fewer porbeagles feeding on them. There is no dispute among the charter skippers and small boat anglers that the mackerel shoals are smaller and patchier now than in the past; apart, that is, from in the very deep water marks way south of the Nab.

A second theory, based on an ecological foundation, is that the porbeagles at the back of the Wight may have been a single family or colony and they might have been cleared out in the past decade. Science has not conclusively established all the patterns of life for sharks, and has not proved that they are migratory, so the bleak possibility that they have been wiped out from behind the Wight does exist.

Shark chartering from all six ports is coupled with an unavoidably long steaming time – between one-and-a-half and three hours. All the boats provide complete sets of sharking equipment – rods, reels, loaded with heavy line, terminal gear and bait. Bait is usually mackerel as they can be caught during the day to ensure absolute freshness, and mainly because they are tremendously oily, which is to the liking of sharks. Usually the skippers will bait up for you, using either a whole mackerel, or various cuts, or even two! The golden rule is that the shark swallows its meal – your mackerel – head first and so hooks must always be facing the tail of the mackerel to ensure a hook hold when the shark takes.

In most cases only three or four shark lines are put out at once, each using a balloon as a very large float. It is common practice for the shark baits to be set at varying depths and at varying distances from the boat – always keeping them in conjunction with the rubby-dubby trail. This is because there are no hard and fast rules about the depths at which shark feed. Feathering for mackerel and noting at which depth they are located should give a possible clue to where the sharks will be feeding.

Getting the rubby-dubby to function successfully is one of the marks of a good skipper. In the waters south of the Island where tides are strong, skippers have the problem of synchronising the direction of drift with the tide and prevailing wind to ensure the rubby-dubby is attracting the sharks. For the angler there is little to do except wait and watch the balloon. The rods carrying the shark lines are leaned against the gunwale with the reels – usually big multipliers – adjusted so that a taking shark will run

(*above*) Chesil Beach, Dorset: a heavy surf washes into Chesil Beach as a party of anglers from Exeter try out the sport at the eastern end where it joins Portland; (*below*) Rock fishing: one moment this ledge was dry and an inviting platform for the angler. The next, this sea set it awash. Great care is needed when choosing a spot for rock fishing

(*above and below*) Hard at it in the good ragworm grounds at Hill Head on the mainland shore of the Solent

out line against the ratchet. Any violent movement of the balloon – sideways, bobbing up or more particularly being taken straight under – gives the first clue to the presence of a shark.

In shark fishing books, the standard theory is to allow the shark its first run, wait for it to turn the bait and swallow it, and then strike to set the hook on its second run. Practice has shown that this system works sometimes, but striking on the first run has also been successful. The only certain fact about shark fishing is that nothing is certain. All the rules are broken, and all the set doctrines are proved wrong at some point. Maybe the golden rule is always to look out for the unexpected. On one shark trip on the Langstone Harbour boat, *Torbay Belle*, the skipper Dave Adams was retrieving the original mackerel bait from the previous day's trip in order to replace it with some fresh that we had just caught. He was handlining the last few feet of trace into the gunwale when a porbeagle made a lunge at the mackerel bait, seizing it almost on the surface, and only a few inches away from his hands. It was a big creature, around the 150lb mark, which eventually dropped the bait after one long run.

Wrecking from this area means reaching the wrecks well south of the Nab Tower – and there the tides are a major factor, sometimes being so fierce that they limit fishing to about two hours at the most. One of the Langstone Harbour boats, *Girl Sharon*, skippered by Dave Steer, has made the most consistent assault on the wrecks, using Decca navigational aids, and has had some trips to rival the west country results. Congers and pollack are the most plentiful species, with up to 500lb of fish being taken in one two-hour spell. Other trips have shown a concentration of tope and spur-dogs around the wrecks – one trip had 40 tope, with red bream, black bream and an occasional cod completing the catches. Fish take conventional wreck-style red-gills and pirks and the favourite sides of mackerel.

6 Chartering in Sussex

Chartering in Sussex is centred on five ports which between them put several dozen boats afloat throughout the year, and which are noted for their great variety of species and quality fish. In West Sussex lies Littlehampton which is internationally famous for its black bream. Shoreham, Brighton Marina and Newhaven lie in central Sussex where their good wrecking is constantly improving. Rye completes the list.

Littlehampton provides charter fishing all the year round but its major attraction is its black bream. It appears that the bream have always congregated off Littlehampton, and one charter skipper, Mike Westlake, has even found references to boats fishing between Littlehampton and Bognor in the eighteenth century when it seems the sport was going strong. Bream are taken in a huge ten-mile radius of Littlehampton; they last longer than elsewhere – from April till late August – and attract anglers from all over Britain.

For a few weeks the bream move into the inshore marks about half a mile off Littlehampton. Here, on what the charter skippers call the Inner Breaming Grounds – an area of chalky bottom to the west of the Harbour entrance – they are thought to spawn. But for the remainder of the time they are caught over a wide area. Rocks produce the best fishing, but are not the only venues. Bream are so thick off Littlehampton that they are even caught in areas between the favourite rock marks – like the Bognor Rocks (to the west), the West and East Ditches, Black Ledge and Kingmere Rocks. These vary in distance from Littlehampton but are less than ten miles – and two hours' steaming time – from the Harbour. Usually the bream are so thick that the charter boats do not need to ground bait for them, although skippers used to keep them feeding over shallower marks with boiled-rice-based rubby-dubby. Generally the rocky areas produce the bigger fish – to 4lb – and some of the best marks are where the bream shoal around rocks covered in a certain kind of weed. While the bream season takes its first tentative steps in April and during the first two weeks of May, it is picking up speed during late May. By June it is running full blast, and some years it lasts well into July or August – with most skippers knowing August hot spots.

In one way the bream hide up the other summer fishing available from Littlehampton, but it is there in strength. Throughout the summer there are large tope packs running through the deep water. Boats travel west to the shoals off Selsey Bill, picking the deep water between the Bill and the Owers Light for tope – which sometimes run over 40lb. Quite often charter boats from Littlehampton encounter sharks. More often than not anglers are smashed by sharks in summer, but a few are landed. Occasionally a boat lays on a shark trip to the back of the Isle of Wight. Through late summer (June and July) and into autumn, Littlehampton's mixed fishing is at its best. Some of the inshore marks yield the common varieties of ray, but each year such trips produce sting ray, turbot and brill. From the inshore marks dabs are plentiful, if only anglers would choose to chase them. A few are usually taken, as it were, by accident, but if the angler was to fish for them, the charter skippers are confident they are there in good numbers. Summer and autumn are good bass fishing periods off Littlehampton Harbour, and in 1976 one netsman, hoping for some early cod, suddenly hit about 500lb of bass in a couple of hauls.

Winter chartering off Littlehampton means whiting galore – and usually some very good cod fishing. The exception was in 1976, when – in keeping with the whole of the charter industry in Sussex and Hampshire – the cod were far thinner on the ground. There were isolated huge fish, and a few large wreck-cod hauls, but in general it was one of the worst cod years in recent memory. Littlehampton – as elsewhere – had the strange compensation of enjoying an influx of huge pollack. Fish of 6lb were exceptional before 1976 off Littlehampton, but then they began being taken up to 14lb. Best places were in the gullies – firstly near the Black Ledge about five miles out; secondly, in the deep water about 11 miles out where the skippers pick up the

Ledge that suddenly drops away to 120ft. This ledge runs through the English Channel along the whole coastline of Sussex, and we will meet it again off Shoreham and Newhaven. The second surprise of 1976, as Mike Westlake pointed out, was the appearance of many light-coloured conger eels where they had never before been caught. The best value of the Littlehampton whiting is that they stay through the winter and linger until February or even April in some deep-water marks.

From Christmas onwards a few sporadic spur-dogs are taken from the deeper water – 80ft to 90ft down – and these catches gradually pick up until the main spur-dog packs arrive in April. Ten years ago, Littlehampton's spur-dogs were nearly as famous as the port's bream when boats would return from the deep literally filled with spurs. Catches are still good as the spurs chase the shoals of sprats through the deep water, and occasionally, when a boat hits one of these packs, an 'old-fashioned' bonanza catch is made. During the winter the skippers can predict what sort of spur-dog season is coming by the actions of the whiting. All the time they are coughing up sprats when caught, the skippers know the spurs will be around. When spur-dog hunting approaches its peak in March and April, the ray fishing is also under way. The variety of ray fishing off Littlehampton includes thornbacks, small-eyed rays, spotted and blondes. By this time the angler's thoughts are usually turning again to the bream.

A major move, begun in the 1970s, within the Shoreham charter industry has had the effect of introducing a new charter force to Sussex – based on Brighton Marina. The formation of the Brighton Marina Boatmen's Association meant a move of several of Shoreham's charter boats together with others from Newhaven, into the new Marina. A fleet of 30 boats is based there and sea anglers have the tremendous facilities of car-parking, a restaurant, a tackle shop, bait supplies and the added bonus of fishing at all states of the tide. This development still leaves a charter fleet in its own right at Shoreham, where some skippers have problems with mud moorings and where they are inconvenienced by being dictated to by the tide. Shoreham's fishing (which is reached by the boats from the new Marina) is renowned for its variety, having both bottom and wreck fishing. In winter the boats take cod, whiting, skate, pout and dogfish. In spring the spur-dogs pack off Shoreham and the rays remain. In summer fishing is at its height; the mackerel move in, bringing in the tope, more skate, bream, pollack (subject to the same increases as elsewhere in 1976), boats hit great summer cod, and congers inhabit the deep-water marks. Skate and pollack remain throughout the autumn, by which time the first whiting are showing as the next winter approaches. Pout, dogfish and huss keep up the sport throughout the year.

Spring for the charter boats off Shoreham means a combination of the last of the winter whiting, still lingering on, with the first spur-dogs being encountered. The same deep ledge off Littlehampton mentioned earlier, runs right along the Shoreham stretch of the Channel and is a major influence. The spur-dog packs build up beyond the Ledge (about 11 miles out where the seabed drops to 120ft). They begin to move in during March and the Shoreham skippers intercept them anywhere from 8 to 11 miles out. Thornbacks and other rays are also on the move during March and April – although a few late frosts in March sometimes deter them.

In late April and May the black bream show. Some boats travel to the west to pick up the eastern end of the Kingmere Rocks that form such a big mark for Littlehampton boats. In addition bream shoal heavily off Shoreham. South-west of Shoreham are the College Rocks that yield bream; they are also taken in the rocky ground along the line of the Ledge. They shoal at their heaviest in late May and June, at the same time that the full variety of Shoreham's fishing is available. About 12 miles out are the Holes – an extremely rocky area with deep gullies interspersed with shale and gravel banks. This is the favourite general area of the skippers. Huge conger (up to 65lb) are taken from the rocks. Big tope run through, chasing the mackerel in summer (tope over 50lb came aboard Mick Gaul's *Sewara* in 1976 for example) and for the skippers who hit shale and gravel patches there are turbot (*Sewara* again had five in one day in the same year). Although none of the Shoreham boats fish for sharks they are seen following the boats every year. If there are anglers on board gutting fish on the way in from wrecking trips during the summer it is not unusual for sharks to follow them in.

Big congers and tope last throughout the autumn when there is an action-replay period of spur-dog activity, after which time the first whiting shoals begin moving. Later in the autumn, from October onwards, the cod come in and are caught regularly for the next three months.

In addition to this wealth of bottom fishing there is a great deal of wrecking. There are reckoned to be 30 or 40 wrecks within the 5½ to 9 mile range of the Shoreham boats, and also within the scope of the Brighton Marina boats. The wrecks traditionally produce pollack, congers, black bream and a few cod. Recently red bream and ling started showing. Some wrecks are well known (like the *Moldavia* about 11 miles out which is heavily fished) while many are known to individual skippers who keep quiet about them. The *Moldavia* is renowned for its big bream in late summer and autumn, while the congers are at their best in summer. The most usual method of fishing these wrecks is for the skipper to anchor up tide and for red-gills to be streamed aft beyond the wreck. Then the anglers retrieve up and across the wreck. It calls for an alert angler prepared to concentrate, especially when the tides are running. Cod are at their best over the wrecks from July to September, with fish topping the 20lb mark often taken.

In contrast to the big fish hunting, Shoreham and Brighton skippers can move to the inshore marks off Rottingdean to the east of Brighton for excellent dab fishing if a northerly wind develops and wipes out the deep-water fishing trips. These inshore trips are a pleasure from Brighton Marina where the running time is very short.

Chartering from Newhaven means more and more wreck fishing nowadays as anglers want to sample the catches of hundredweights of wreck cod, pollack, mighty conger, black and red bream, and ling. Basically, wreck fishing off Newhaven is divided into deep-water wrecking (about 15 to 18 miles out on wrecks lying in 30 fathoms of water) or the moderate-distance wrecks (within an eight-mile radius of Newhaven).

With the combination of World War I, World War II and storm casualties, it is reckoned by one of the port's most experienced skippers, Bob Macnamara, that there are between 200 and 300 wrecks in the area. The one major disadvantage with wrecking here, which leaves it a little less attractive than wrecking in the west country, is that the tides are very strong – giving the skippers a more difficult time in settling over the wrecks and anglers a harder time fishing them than their west country counterparts. Anglers chartering from Newhaven can expect to be using 2lb of lead all the time while wrecking and more when the tide gets going. Wire line is useful. Wrecking gets under way in May when pollack, pout, ling and conger start feeding hard, and later, in June, the black bream shoals join in. They ensure that a steady stream of fish is coming aboard – even if they are the smaller species – while the angler is waiting for the big individual conger. Many wreck bream reach the 4lb mark. Later in the season, towards August, some red bream feed over the wrecks – though not in such good numbers.

The most exciting aspect of the wrecks is when shoals of cod come in towards the end of March. They are fish which have finished spawning and which are hungry. As they shoal and feed greedily, anglers take them in good numbers on pirks. Some wreck concentrations here are tremendous. In one area just over 15 miles out, most of an entire convoy is thought to have suffered during World War II and about 18 wrecks litter the seabed in a five-mile area. Immediately off Newhaven – inside a ten-mile radius enabling fixes to be taken from landmarks – there are 35 wrecks. Several wrecks are inshore. The *Brisbane*, *Lancer* and *Celtic* are about three miles off and provide all the smaller wreck species. In contrast, the deep-water wrecks hold huge fish and Newhaven has had its share of congers to 70lb.

Newhaven has some great mixed fishing as its second attraction. One favourite mark is off the Ledge (the same seabed fault that we have seen before) which is between eight and ten miles out where the bottom drops away to 27 fathoms. In winter, good catches of spur-dogs are taken in the deep water over the Ledge, together with cod, bull huss, tope, dogs and rays throughout the year. In contrast there are many inshore marks which provide small-fish potential. Plaice, dabs and codling are taken off the Portobello Pipe almost as far west as Saltdean or off Old Nore Point (immediately west of Newhaven) by anglers using worm. Newhaven and Brighton Marina skippers all have prolific whiting marks for the winter in this area. They sometimes use the very best weather conditions in summer to motor east to Beachy Head where they find rich tope runs a few miles off the Head. Throughout the summer these Beachy Head areas also provide black bream.

Rye has a charter business on a smaller scale than the other four ports and its skippers have a more difficult problem with the very tidal and shallower harbour. But it too offers great variety with plenty of wreck fishing out deep in a very busy section of the English Channel. It has strong cod and whiting fishing in winter – especially to the east off Dungeness and in other Kent waters – and with inshore potential in Rye Bay.

Deep-water wrecking off Rye means fishing in the heart of the main English Channel shipping lanes to the south-east off Dungeness Point. Many of the skippers use the buoys separating the shipping lanes as marks (although they point out wryly that the separation buoys don't always keep the east- and west-bound ships apart). To the charter skippers it is no surprise that the area has a decent supply of wrecks. These produce pollack and big congers, with really big eels over 60lb coming from the wrecks further east. Rye boats pick up a great variety of fish in deep waters with spur-dogs in spring and for a few weeks in autumn, tope in summer (once again running very big), big shoals of mackerel and black bream in summer, and large pout, bull huss and dogfish all the time.

Some wrecks lie in shallower water, as close as six miles out in Rye Bay. Deep-water marks also include several areas of rock which provide Rye boats with their main variety. While the rocks themselves produce more congers, pollack, bream, mackerel, tope, huss, dogfish, spurs and pout, the sandy areas around them yield plaice and even turbot. The whole area produces rays which begin in late March and April and which last until the winter. For its inshore fishing Rye Bay produces many more flatfish marks, with plaice and dabs to be had in large numbers and with whiting in winter. Many of the charter skippers regard this kind of fishing as a substitute when bad weather wipes out deep-water fishing. Anglers who are prepared to adapt and go after the flatfish can take great catches. During the winter, the big cod – which frequently top the 25lb mark – are the main target for anglers out of Rye. The cod season starts in October, has its peak between then and December, and continues with lone fish being caught through till March.

7 Inshore Fishing in Small Boats

Getting afloat in private boats − some big, some small dinghies − is an enormous sport along the central southern coast. It is basically the sport of 'locals' living along the coast who flock out in their thousands in armadas of boats. Their numbers are swelled by visitors who are prepared to tow boats from miles inland to sample the excellent inshore fishing available. In the Solent and Spithead and the waters around the Isle of Wight, the south boasts one of the busiest and most prolific fishing grounds for private boats, while Weymouth and Poole in the west and Eastbourne and Hastings in East Sussex sport large fleets of small boats.

The two biggest factors governing the use of private boats are the number of fish in an area and its predominant weather conditions. Central southern England has plenty of the country's top fishing (see Chapter 2) for bass and flatfish along the whole of the 200 or more miles of coastline from Lyme Regis to Rye, and in their own seasons as good cod, whiting, tope, spur-dog, smoothhound and ray fishing as anywhere in Britain. But from a weather viewpoint the net result is not such good news. The Solent area and Spithead enjoy the marvellous shelter of the Isle of Wight − the greatest single factor making the area the most heavily fished from small boats − but elsewhere, small-boat anglers are exposed to the English Channel and its often violent moods. Boats out of Weymouth enjoy some protection from Portland Bill when the wind is from the predominant south-west, and the peninsulas of St Alban's Head and Durlston Head afford the same protection for boats out of Poole fishing Poole Bay. But for the remainder of the coastline the natural wind-swept state of the Channel has a strong influence on the numbers of anglers afloat. Even if the wind has died off over the Channel, the sea often displays a heavy swell, always bearing testimony to the blow that has just passed.

An enormous variety of private boats are used in the south, united in the common bond that their design will have catered for heavy sea conditions. You need a good sea-boat for Channel work. Fibre-glass boats are becoming increasingly popular but 'locals' will tell you you cannot beat a heavy clinker-built sea-boat. Along most of the coastline anglers can expect to have to contend with a long swell − a point worth remembering when contemplating what size of boat to buy. In the Solent, on the other hand, there is a nearly unique, choppy, short sea that needs a different consideration.

Sport in the south is prolific, no matter what size of boat your purse will reach − be it a 30ft inboard-engined cruiser, a 16ft outboard-engined boat or a 10ft rowing dinghy. Between Lyme Regis and Rye the angler has a choice of every kind of seabed to fish and most species of fish to catch, all within a mile or two of the shore − and in many cases within hundreds of yards of the beach. Sussex and the eastern end of central southern England have excellent sandy bottoms for plaice and dabs, and fine rocky areas for bass. Hampshire is renowned for some of its flounder venues. Both Sussex and Hampshire figure prominently in cod catches in winter and black bream catches in summer. Throughout the south there are patches of rock available for the small-boat owner to fish. In Dorset these produce some excellent pollack fishing. Rough areas of ground which produce mixed fishing are widely scattered. In the Solent in a small rowing boat in 1976 I took six species on one day (smoothhound, thornback ray, spotted ray, dogfish, bass and pout) and from Spithead eight or nine species are regularly caught on individual trips. Last year a boat returned from a trip off Weymouth with 16 species aboard.

No matter what size boat you use, there is a whole range of safety precautions, necessary equipment, together with common-sense rules to ensure your safety at sea. Before going afloat, always check the two natural factors − tides and the weather. Always heed weather forecasts. There are many anglers who have been caught out in gales and storms which have sprung up after a calm beginning to a day. Had they listened to the forecasts they could have spared themselves anxious times − or even worse consequences. On the BBC shipping forecast the areas to listen out for are 'Dover, Wight, Portland and Plymouth'. While Dover (in the east), Wight (centred on Hampshire), and Portland (to the west) will give you immediate conditions, you can arm yourself with prior warning of bad weather coming in from the west by listening to and remembering the Fastnet, Sole and Finesterre and the west country forecasts. What is with them today, could reach you 100 miles along the south coast tomorrow. Another invaluable aid is local knowledge. There are many instances where such knowledge is the best advice available – and weather is one. It is the old chap sitting on the sea wall who can tell you from the ring round the sun that there's a storm brewing, or from the small black clouds scudding in from the back of the Island that rain squalls are on the way. Take the trouble to ask him – and pay heed to what he says. Similarly, tides are a factor that you can account for in advance. Tides have a direct bearing on whether or not you fish, and dictate precisely how you fish and what species you can expect to catch. Prior consultation with tide charts will tell you whether you are arriving at a beach at low water or high, whether launching your dinghy will therefore be a simple matter or a back-breaker. More to the point, a glance at a tide chart will tell you if you can get to your boat in its harbour, or whether it is high and dry on the low-water mud. The effect of tides on fishing is far more important. Central southern England is subject to very strong tides. Portland Race is infamous for violent tides. The races through the Needles, through the West Solent and off Beachy Head are fierce and often dangerous. Tides all round the Isle of Wight – especially off the south-east point of Dunnose – are so strong that fishing is sometimes impossible. When tides are in control they can be disruptive, but by careful planning the angler can turn them to his advantage. He can plan trips to coincide with the best tides when he will be able to fish as the tide slackens, through its slack period, and through the period as it picks up speed again. More precisely he can fish when certain fish are known to feed at certain states of the tide – particularly flatfish. Getting a working knowledge of the tides is vital and there are three sources to draw from – detailed tidal information is given on Admiralty charts; the angler can purchase tide-chart books; and as a last resort he can again consult the local knowledge of those around him.

For any angler fishing inshore waters regularly, Admiralty charts are invaluable. Most tackle dealers should be able to tell you where you can buy them. On each chart you will find a box of what appear to be mathematical equations. It is, in fact, a very precise and detailed analysis of the tidal direction, strength and timing for the area of the chart. At the top of each box you will find a diamond shape enclosing a letter. Look across the chart and you will find the diamond symbol somewhere at sea. The tidal details below the diamond in the box refer to the particular spot where that lettered diamond is fixed at sea. In the extreme left-hand column of figures the angler is told how many hours before or after high water the reading was taken (and each box tells you which high-water location is being used). The second column tells the angler the direction of the tide (on a compass bearing) at each separate time, and the third column tells him the strength. Armed with the knowledge of what time high water is expected, and the Admiralty chart for the area, the angler can precisely calculate the tide direction – when it is slack, when it is gathering momentum and when it will be running full bore.

A book of tide charts gives him the same information as a series of diagrams of the area, each showing it at hourly intervals, with arrows and tide strengths indicating how the direction and flow alter during the tide's cycle. Again the angler needs to know the time of high tide from which he can again calculate the exact conditions of the tide throughout the day.

Local knowledge on tides is vital. It is only the local who knows that the fish feed off one beach two hours after low water, but that they feed over that gulley two hours before high. Eventually, after fishing often enough in an area you will acquire your own experience – but until you reach that stage, seek out and consult the locals. For those who fish from rowing boats – often the most vulnerable of dinghies – remember what a powerful influence the tide is. Always plan fishing trips so that you will be rowing home at the end of the day either with the tide or on slack tide. I have spent many a weary evening battling back across the Solent against a foul tide, getting ever more tired as the yards have slowly dragged by.

The next safety consideration is equipment. The same rules apply about personal equipment as when going afloat on a charter boat. Be warm, with waterproof gear to keep you dry, and remember that in small dinghies the golden rule is 'never stand up'. Be fully dressed before you go afloat in small dinghies. Trying to don extra jumpers and trousers and large coats while afloat in a tender dinghy with a sea running is no fun. Always carry a compass. In small boats even a pocket compass is sufficient, but you should *never* go afloat without one. Even on the shortest trip – a few hundred yards off your local beach – you can be subject to sudden sea mists or even dense fog. Always carry at least one distress flare; or in the case of larger boats, several flares. A fully comprehensive network of coastguard stations and lifeboat facilities are laid on along the south coast waiting to give assistance the moment you get into difficulties. Remember, they are powerless to help unless you can attract their attention. If your trip is lasting into darkness, take a good light – either a lamp or torch or both – as a safety factor. They are not needed so much for you to see by, but rather to enable others to see you. Always take reserve means of propulsion. Take extra fuel, and keep a pair of oars aboard if you are fishing from a motor boat. If you own a rowing boat keep a spare oar in it in case one snaps. Because much of the best inshore fishing along the south coast is found on rocky grounds – the black bream haunts off Littlehampton or off the eastern seaboard of the Isle of Wight, or the conger and pollack lairs off Dorset – small-boat owners can expect to have the problem of making anchors hold in rocks. Making them hold is often the easy part. It is when you come to breaking them out that anchors can present a safety problem. The safest and most simple trick is to trip your anchor. This means tying the anchor rope to the fluke with a comparatively weak twine or cord. If the initial pressure fails to dislodge an anchor from its hold, intense pressure will snap the trip, and you are then, in effect, pulling from a different direction – and this usually frees the anchor. If that still fails, then the importance of a knife as a piece of safety equipment becomes apparent. Imagine that you have dropped your anchor in rock and it is jammed. The weather is deteriorating, or a fog is coming in, or perhaps a large vessel is approaching straight and fast. Getting the anchor out is vital. If it becomes downright dangerous, the last resort is to cut yourself free. With a knife you have a chance; without one, you could be in real trouble. With anchors being expensive items, there is one trick which can save you its loss even in circumstances such as these. Instead of permanently securing the anchor to your boat, have an anchor warp far longer than you would normally use and attach a buoy to the other end. In the event of the anchor becoming impossibly stuck, you can throw over the rope and buoy – effectively freeing you from the anchor, and allowing you the chance to return at a later date to retrieve it.

The essence of private boat fishing in inshore waters is to be completely self-supporting. First priority is to remember all the aforementioned safety equipment. Next there are the major fishing items that you will need – charter anglers can leave those to the skipper. If you are expecting the smaller species – bass, flatfish, bream – carry a landing net. If you are chasing the bigger fish – skate, congers, bull huss – carry a gaff. To be safe, carry both. Take a baler no matter how calm it is, as there are many ways of shipping water. Take a bucket or fish box or large polythene bag to accommodate the fish; always try to drop the fish straight into the containers to avoid getting scales and slime all over the boat. If you are expecting to meet conger eels, a sack or length of sacking is useful in a small boat. Some large eels have come from inshore rocky patches off the Dorset coast and the Isle of Wight coasts. Sacking quickly relieves a conger of its slime and quietens it down. The lack of a sack or a knife to dispatch a conger quickly has led to some anxious moments in small dinghies. This is the second use of the knife – as a piece of fishing equipment. A sharp knife helps with precise bait presentation when fishing with fish strips, and also helps with speedy and neat knot-tying when tackling up or changing or replacing terminal gear. A priest takes up little room and is invaluable for most of the mixed species found in the south. With dogfish, bull huss, spur-dogs and smoothhounds it helps enormously – especially in a very small dinghy – to be able to dispatch the fish instantly. Your priest or 'bodger, bonker or dispatcher' need not be elaborate. Anything will do. Having forgotten mine, I once used a lemonade bottle successfully. One small word of warning – when wielding a priest in a fibre-glass boat, beware of smashing the hull – you could damage it without much effort!

Your fishing tackle needs to be as comprehensive as that of the charter angler – and it does no harm to carry tackle for other methods of fishing in addition to that which you intend to use. Something unexpected could crop up – a sudden passing shoal of mackerel or a few marauding tope – upon which you could capitalise if your tackle box is fully equipped.

One modern trend among private boat owners nowadays is to buy slightly larger boats with more powerful engines in order to travel to deeper waters. One piece of equipment which is purely a fishing aid is an echo-sounder, which can cost anything between about fifty and several hundred pounds. It really boils down to the angler choosing between his next set of tackle – a full set of rods, reels, and gear could cost that much – or an echo-sounder. The sounder is invaluable, and anglers who have them often wonder how they ever managed to catch fish before. In general, if you are fishing very close inshore where fixes from easily visible landmarks can help you pinpoint a mark and find it again, the echo-sounder is not so essential. But if you are travelling to deeper water marks further offshore, where fixes are impracticable, the sounder will help you find exact marks. Its main function is to give you a precise picture of the seabed, and thus help you locate the fish. Most fish feed where there is a sudden variation in depth – in deep gullies, down the sides of banks or over uneven rocks. The most obvious use of the echo-sounder is for locating wrecks where 10 or 20yd off the mark could be crucial. Your local knowledge and land fixes will put you near a mark – say a rocky shoal – to within a few hundred yards. You could then anchor on the 90yd of flat unbroken ground around. With an echo-sounder you can fish on the precise ledge on the 10yd target spot. On target you will catch fish, while other boats in that 90yd off-target radius will miss them. When using an echo-sounder in a small boat one must remember that it works by recording the distance between the boat and the seabed. This means that if a big sea is running and the boat is rising and falling with the waves, the echo-sounder will show an undulating seabed which could be misleading.

The cheaper echo-sounders are depth-sounder types which have a circular face calibrated in fathoms and feet or metres. Depth is shown by a light appearing against the scale. These are useful and prices range from about £50 upwards. More expensive echo-sounders – those that give a paper-roll print-out of the bottom – are even more useful, giving a virtual picture of the seabed, and clearly showing rocks and wrecks. These cost upwards of £200. Although they really require an outside source of power, they can be used in quite small boats off a 12-volt motor-cycle battery. The equipment consists of the sounder which records the impulses bounced back off the bottom after being sent out by the transducer. This looks like a long-handled torch, and operates simply by having its face actually in the water to emit its signal. Because the equipment is expensive, most anglers like to take it with them from boat to new boat, so it is important to have the appropriate fixtures which will allow it to be removed. One Solent small-boat enthusiast who has done just this is David Elbourn who has devised, used and tested four methods of temporary transducer fixtures – all of which work efficiently. The fifth method is for a permanent fixture.

(1) *Plain bracket*
Make an aluminium U-shaped bracket with a hole in one end to take the face of the transducer, and a slot in the other to take its stem. Use the nuts on the transducer stem to lock it into the slot at the appropriate height. The whole bracket can be screwed to the stern so that the face of the transducer is level with the bottom of the hull.

(2) *Stick mounting*
Take a length of wood and bore out a hole at one end to take the transducer. Cut a slot to hold the stem and cable. This is then attached to the stern by means of an aluminium or stainless steel bracket (to hold the lower end against water pressure) and a G-cramp at the top, screwed to the piece of wood and cramped to the transom.

With both these methods it is safer, as your boat runs into the beach, to take the transducer out of its holder to avoid smashing it against the beach on landing.

(3) *Plastic pipe*
Surprisingly enough, a satisfactory echo can be recorded through a glass-reinforced plastic hull by laminating a plastic pipe inside the hull below the water line. Fill the pipe with water and place the transducer inside. Provided there are no metal fittings on the boat beneath the transducer, it will work.

86

(*above*) Poole Harbour: just one corner of this enormous harbour illustrates the vast potential for the angler. Here is a view with Brownsea Island (right) and Sandbanks (to the left); (*below*) Weymouth, Dorset: some of the charter fleet moored in Weymouth Harbour awaiting the day's anglers

(*above* and *below*) West Bay, Bridport, Dorset: West Bay's inner harbour showing how beautifully protected it is from the predominant south-westerlies blowing in the Channel

(4) *Hand-holder*

Bore a hole in the bottom piece of wood to hold the transducer. Bore a hole in the top piece to take the stem. Screw the two halves together, add a suitable handle and insert the transducer.

Of course there are anglers who have settled into a boat and who will want their echo-sounder fixed permanently.

(5) *Permanent fixture*

Bore a hole in the hull to take the stem only. Shape a piece of wood with a hole bored to take the transducer. Fasten this to the outer hull. Lock the transducer in place with the nuts on the stem.

Small-boat owners along the south coast can derive great benefit from the numerous clubs that exist. They provide slipways with access to the sea to augment public slipways, they provide compounds where boats may be kept, usually close to the sea, and which provide some degree of protection from the ever-growing problem of theft and vandalism. Clubs provide a wealth of anglers with local knowledge who can pool information and make available to the newcomer a bank of experience upon which to draw. They are focal points for anglers, and even if you go out alone, the chances are that you will find club members around the slipway to help you back in with your boat. You are not obliged to take part in competitions. Many anglers, interested only in the excitement of the catch and beating the fish, shun the idea of beating fellow anglers – but competitions can be useful. If there are club members who regularly do well, the reason is that they are fishing better than you. Try to use matches to your advantage. Learn what the others did which gave them better catches – not just so that you can beat them next time, but rather to improve and expand your fishing knowledge.

8 Inshore Fishing West of Portland

To the west of Portland Bill is the wide arc of Lyme Bay, sweeping down into Devon and ultimately round to the south-west past Brixham and Dartmouth to Start Point. The Dorset half of Lyme Bay, from its western extremity at Lyme Regis to Portland Bill, is the more exposed section, lying wide open to fierce south-westerly winds. For this reason it is not such a busy stretch of the coast for small-boat fishing as, say, the Solent's sheltered waters further east. But the boats that go out find good sport over predominantly rocky areas. Most of the small-boat work is done out of West Bay Harbour at Bridport, from Lyme Regis in the west and to a lesser degree from points off Chesil Beach, particularly Chesil Cove at the Portland Bill end of the famous Beach. The most popular and frequently caught fish are pollack, wrasse and conger (throughout the mass of rocky marks), bass (for which many boats troll), pout (everywhere) and thornback rays and whiting (predominantly in the winter).

Lyme Bay's inshore fishing has a Dorset atmosphere about it, with great clifflands at the back of the bay, rocky headlands, and fishing over rock ledges and individual rocks. Part of that atmosphere is the instinctive safety factor of keeping one eye on the weather. By the time waves have built up across the 50-odd miles of Lyme Bay when pushed hard by a south-westerly wind, they provide a tremendous ground swell on the shingle beaches. This is very dangerous, and often impossible for launching and landing small boats. It is most noticeable along the whole of Chesil Beach – about 17 miles of shingle, which is subject to almost constant heavy surf. Although a major feature when considering the benefits to the beach angler (see Chapter 16) the surf means that boat fishing by launching from Chesil is often impossible. Here, the heavy surf is not confined to winter, as the south-west wind prevails all year round. But in winter, especially after Christmas and through January and February, most of the small-boat fishing ceases completely. The sea conditions become an important safety factor from the biggest port on this stretch of coastline, West Bay Harbour at Bridport.

Although Bridport is the name on the lips of the visitors, it actually lies about two miles inland, and they are in fact travelling to West Bay which is the harbour and beach, being at the very western end of Chesil Beach. The harbour entrance consists of two large stone piers shielding a narrow channel leading into a larger rectangular basin. When strong winds are blowing from the south-west, an unmanageable swell builds up in the channel, making a treacherous situation for small boats. Even a medium breeze produces difficult conditions. The harbour entrance is almost dry and certainly not navigable at low water. When the wind swings to the west – still producing difficult conditions along most of this stretch – the shelter afforded to inshore marks immediately west of Lyme Regis makes them about the safest place to fish.

Immediately to the west of Lyme Regis is Pinhay Bay and about three quarters of a mile offshore lie the Pinhay Rocks. These offer two opportunities for the angler – to bottom fish for conger, bull huss, wrasse and pout, or to drift for pollack. When bottom fishing, the greatest success is often met by anglers using a flowing trace, either legered or paternostered. While the bigger species take mackerel (whole, half or fillet) herring or whole squid, the smaller species take ragworm. Moving west from Pinhay Bay towards Lyme Regis itself, feathering accounts for good catches of mackerel. Further outside, between one and two miles offshore, are several marks – including a wreck – which provide conger, bull huss and skate fishing, with freshly caught mackerel as choice bait, and herring as a reserve.

To the east of Lyme Regis is Broad Ledge, which is a welcome refuge where boat anglers can at least fish for the day, if the offshore marks are blown off by the weather. Smaller species, mostly pollack, wrasse and pout are most often taken, with prawn being used to full advantage. Broad Ledge itself is one of the better grounds for catching prawns; the locals often go out in dinghies using drop-nets baited with old fish heads or mackerel. The prawns are then used live, and are particularly effective for bass.

Further east – almost as far along as Charmouth – a rocky ledge stands out from the cliffs for about 400yd, which is a busy ground for the smaller species.

As it extends further out, it becomes broken and spread with individual rocks and platforms. Again, pollack, wrasse, bull huss and pout fall to the anchored boats – with an occasional conger coming from particularly rocky sections in the broken ground on the offshore tip of the ledge. There are two more options open to the boat angler over this mark. He can drift-line with worm or live prawn (particularly killing for bass and pollack) or up anchor and troll a red-gill over an area around the rocky ledge. The secret of success when trolling is to allow the red-gill a very long flowing trace for maximum movement.

The next rocky ledge is a larger ridge with bigger individual rocks off the Golden Gap cliffs between Charmouth and Seatown. These huge clifflands overshadow the tiny village of Seatown to the east, and the rocky ledge which begins beneath them extends out for nearly a mile. This ledge – heavily weed-covered – provides a chance for bigger congers, as well as the usual rock species, wrasse, pollack and pout. At the outside end of the ridge – in more than 30ft of water – thornbacks, bull huss and dogfish are taken. When fishing for the conger here, a wire trace is necessary to beat the fish's sharp teeth. Tackle losses can be expected in this rough, rocky and heavily weeded area. Feathering for mackerel is productive in this area during the summer to provide bait – and if the feathers are switched to red-gills, or if the larger feathers are used, pollack can also be taken.

Further south-west from the Golden Gap ledge lies a mark where the same species are taken – but usually larger specimens. This applies especially to the pout, which will feed even on the large mackerel baits intended for the good conger and huss. From the inshore end of Golden Gap ledge to the east are various areas of shallow water between rocky patches which hold bass. East Ebb Cove, a shallow rocky area near Thorncombe Beacon to the east of Seatown is one such point. Throughout this area good clues to where the rockiest areas lie are the lobster-pot markers put down by professional commercial fishermen. Whereas it is a sensible aid to your fishing to be guided to the rocks by the pot markers, do not go too close. You stand the risk of getting pot ropes round your propeller – and you will ruin the fisherman's pot equipment. Some anglers in small dinghies are tempted to moor to pot-marker buoys. This should never be done, as you could easily damage the pots themselves by dragging them over the rocks.

To the east of the outside end of Golden Gap Ledge about three quarters of a mile directly off Seatown village are the Stile Grounds, which attract thornbacks and dogfish, and which improve in winter when the whiting come in, but further east between Seatown and Eype Point are even better mixed fishing grounds stretching further out to sea.

With the beach at Seatown and along this stretch of coast being particularly vulnerable to the prevailing south-westerlies, few boats put out from along here for the marks outside. They are mostly fished by boats coming out of West Bay, Bridport, three miles further along to the east. Most boat anglers out of Bridport who turn to the west are looking for rocky ground where they can hunt pollack and bass – with deeper offshore rock marks yielding the bigger species – conger and bull huss. Some of these marks for this kind of fishing lie almost as far west as Seatown.

The inshore set of rocks are west of Thorncombe Beacon which sits above Eype Rocks on the coast, while the outer rocks, spread over a larger area that extends for up to two miles further south, yield all the bigger species, conger, skate, huss, pollack, wrasse and pouting. These rocks are a prime example of where the angler can use the lobster-pot marker buoys for guidance. Anglers fishing out of West Bay and aiming at these rocks should always remember the constant potential for the weather to change quickly across Lyme Bay. One again it is best to be guided by local weather knowledge and heed local forecasts if you are going to fish these further rocks. Between the two patches of rock off Seatown is a sandy area which produces whiting in autumn and winter – though the weather usually means that it is not fished very heavily.

Far busier are the rough and rocky areas nearer West Bay Harbour itself, about three quarters of a mile from the harbour and not quite as far west as Eype Point. These are most popular, being within range of small dinghies and yet still yielding the main rock species – pollack, wrasse, conger, pout and bull huss.

Most boats are after pollack over these rocky areas, known as the Pollack Grounds, and drift-lining a long trace with prawn or mackerel strip takes pollack successfully. Mackerel are plentiful through this area, and feathering at the beginning of the day's fishing should provide bait for the day. Feathering and trolling often takes pollack with the mackerel, and mackerel baits fished large on the bottom take conger and bass.

East of West Bay Harbour is Chesil Beach. Some small-boat fishing is carried out by the locals who find rock fishing from Burton Bradstock and Swyre at the Bridport end of the Chesil Beach, and Abbotsbury further to the east. Probably the busiest small-boat section of all is at Chesil Cove, where boats moving south towards the tip of Portland Bill find the usual rock species over rocky patches there. But anyone in a boat fishing this area must bear in mind that just a little further south is the treacherous Portland Race, which will in effect 'suck' him south in the tide if he is careless. This is the time to consult local knowledge about the tides − and the dangers they present.

9 Inshore Fishing:
Portland to the Solent

Between Portland Bill in Dorset and the Hurst Spit entrance to
the Solent in Hampshire, the southern coast is divided into areas
of heavy concentrations of small fishing boats, and long sections
where small-boat fishing is impossible. Basically, to the west –
apart from a concentration at Weymouth and a smaller element
at Lulworth – the area was not fashioned with the small-boat
man in mind. Further east, starting at Swanage and flourishing at
Poole and through beyond Christchurch, the area belongs very
much to the boat angler.

From Portland Bill to the twin headlands of St Alban's Head
and Durlston Head, the majestic sheer Dorset cliffs and downs
reach to the sea – all very wonderful for the lover of scenery, but
of no use to the angler seeking a launching spot for his boat. He
must travel as far as Weymouth where he has launching
facilities, and good fishing within range. But beware, never think
of taking a small boat towards the Portland Race off Portland
Bill. You will hear tales of glorious bass fishing – and they are
true – but not for small boats. For safety's sake, forget the
notion of working the Race with a small boat. Without travelling
so far as the Bill, Portland offers a great deal of fishing for the
boat owner out of Weymouth – with good marks in range both
inside Portland Harbour and outside its man-made breakwaters.
Fishing inside Portland Harbour is basically divided into three
types – the bass fishing done through most of the harbour, the
pollack, bream, wrasse and conger fishing around its breakwaters
and the flatfishing done to the west on the shore side.

In dramatic contrast to the fierce tides of the Race a few miles
south, the harbour has little tidal movement, so bass fishing is
mostly done by trolling with live sandeels or live prawns. Inside
Portland Harbour is the tidal entrance to the Fleet at Ferrybridge

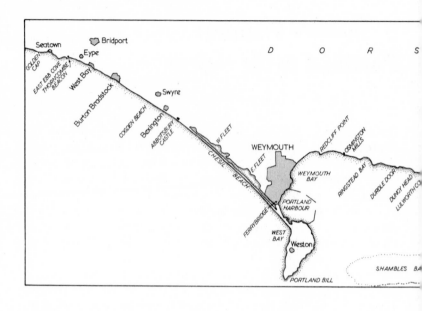

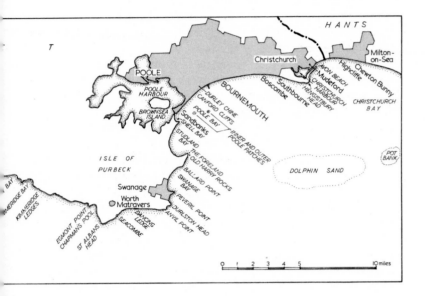

HANTS

POOLE

Christchurch

Milton-
on-Sea

POOLE
HARBOUR

BROWNSEA
ISLAND

BOURNEMOUTH

DURLEY CHINE
CANFORD CLIFFS
POOLE BAY

Boscombe

Southbourne

AVON BEACH
Mudeford
CHRISTCHURCH
HARBOUR
HENGISTBURY
HEAD

Highcliffe

Chewton Bunny

CHRISTCHURCH
BAY

Sandbanks
SHELL BAY
ST ALDHELM
BAY

ISLE OF
PURBECK

INNER AND OUTER
POOLE PATCHES

POT
BANK

THE FORELAND
OLD HARRY ROCKS

DOLPHIN SAND

BALLARD POINT
SWANAGE
BAY

Swanage

BAY

KIMMERIDGE LEDGES

EGMONT POINT
CHAPMAN'S POOL
ST ALBANS
HEAD

Worth
Matravers

PEVERIL POINT
DURLSTON HEAD
ANVIL POINT

DANCING
LEDGE
SEACOMBE

0 1 2 3 4 5   10 miles

– giving the lie to the general belief that the Fleet or Littlesea behind Chesil Beach is a land-locked lake. The Fleet entrance at Ferrybridge produces the only strong tide inside the harbour. Although it is a place to avoid when the tide is flooding into the Fleet, when it is ebbing it gives the bass fisherman a chance to stop trolling and drift-line instead.

Trolling, drifting or legering near the great breakwaters will take pollack and bass, although small fish – pout, small bream and wrasse – will often beat the better fish to the bait. The angler, hunting with big baits – lasks of mackerel or herring – should find the conger near the breakwater, but he must be prepared to lose some tackle in obstructions or weed on the breakwaters. Plaice and flounders can both be taken on the shore side of the harbour, both on the Weymouth and Portland Bill sides of the Ferrybridge entrance to the Fleet.

In Weymouth Bay itself most anglers head for two similar rocky ledges at Redcliff Point (which is a small ledge) and further east at Ringstead Ledge (which is more prominent). Both produce mixed fishing of both small species (bream, pout, dogfish, wrasse, bass and pollack) and larger species (congers, huss, skate). If you intend to travel to the further Ringstead mark, keep one eye on the weather, as the return journey into a south-westerly wind could get choppy and become lengthy.

That wonderful cliffland scenic beauty of Dorset takes over for the next few miles of coast – to the exclusion of the boat angler – until Lulworth Cove is reached when the angler finds more launching access facilities. Although there are good fishing marks around Lulworth Cove, the small-boat traffic is light because of the inherent dangers. Good bass and pollack drift-lining and trolling exists to the east in Worbarrow Bay and even further east in Kimmeridge Bay, and both bays contain rocky grounds that hold quantities of large conger, huss and pollack – but their distance from an access point puts them practically out of range of the small-boat man.

Nearer to Lulworth are the Lulworth Banks which lie about two miles off and which stretch from off Lulworth to the west. These include rough areas – rocky broken ground giving pollack, wrasse and dogfish, with occasional congers – and the remainder of the banks which give rays and flatfish, and occasional tope. Even these banks can be far enough out for the small dinghy man if the weather turns nasty. It must always be remembered that along this stretch of coast, the weather plays sudden tricks. Further inshore off Lulworth Cove – between the Cove and Durdle Door to the west – there are good trolling and spinning grounds for mackerel and pollack.

It is between these points off Lulworth and the easternmost part of Durlston Head that the sheer cliff faces with rocks beneath and strong tides mean that the small-boat man must keep clear. But round the point at Durlston the picture changes. From Swanage, and mostly from Poole, small boats flood out to good fishing grounds covering miles of sea.

Immediately south of Swanage is Peveril Point, and to the north, across Swanage Bay is Ballard Down. Between them they provide an effective wind-break, sheltering the Bay from the prevailing south-westerly winds, and thus giving small boats a chance to fish in all but the strongest east winds. Tides generally are not too strong – except for those boats which venture south of Peveril Point and out, for example, off Anvil Point Lighthouse, where there are rocks holding big congers, pollack, wrasse and bull huss. But from Peveril Point northwards, the area is a mass of fishing marks. Immediately east of the Point there is good tope and skate fishing to be had, while trolling the ledge itself which runs out from Peveril Point produces pollack, mackerel and wrasse.

Swanage Bay itself has several rocky ledges and rock patches which produce bream, pollack and bass. The greatest asset of these marks is that they are close inside the bay and within the reach of small dinghies. In the northern corner of Swanage Bay towards Ballard Down this is particularly true, with rough broken ground yielding bass, bream and pollack in quite shallow waters. One good mark off the two caves at Ballard Down produces the best bream within 40yd and 100yd of the beach.

Going further north from Ballard towards the Old Harry Rocks, the angler is moving into the waters fished mostly by Poole-based boats, rather than Swanage boats. The Old Harry Rocks themselves produce the famous bream in summer – but for the angler who wants a change there is an old wreck, blown up and fragmented about 1½ miles east of the Rocks, which yields congers. North of Headfast Point (overlooking the Old

Harry Rocks) is Studland Bay, which enjoys the same sheltering effect that Swanage experiences.

Studland Bay holds plenty of flatfish – mainly flounders, dabs and plaice, with the occasional turbot and even brill – which can be taken both on the drift under the shelter of Headfast Point, or from at anchor. The bass fishing in the north of Studland Bay is more accurately a continuation of the bass fishing out of the entrance to Poole Harbour. From the southern corner of Shell Haven running south-east is the man-made Training Bank which is partially covered at its deeper end at high tide, about three quarters of a mile offshore. Its other extremity is marked by the Training Bank Beacon and round this point, and on both sides of the bank, there is excellent trolling for bass and pollack especially for the angler with live sandeels or live pout for bait. Between the Training Bank Beacon and the bank itself, and moving south into the Bar Sands area of Studland Bay, fishing a baited spoon accounts for plaice. Plaice also congregate on the Hooks Sands on the northern side of the Swash – the main flow out of Poole Harbour. These plaice are taken from April through the summer and occasionally as late as autumn. Sometimes the bass fishing from the Swash is tremendous, especially if the angler gives the fish a chance. Try drift-lining live sandeels or a live pout with no weight at all on a long flowing trace, to about 8lb line. The result shows up the bass in its finest colours.

To the east of the harbour entrance, off Branksome Chine, are the three patches of rock which are conveniently within the range of small boats – especially the Inner Poole Patch. This produces mostly pout, while the Outer Poole Patch produces much better mixed fishing. These rocks also take things – like anchors from the unwary, so tripping your anchor here is a necessity. Locating the rocks is made easier by the lobster fishermen who leave them well marked with lobster-pot buoys. Further to the east off Durley Chine are more marks within range of the Poole boats, but there are also launching facilities from Durley Chine – reached by a road, with a car park – which swell the numbers fishing here. A favourite mark is the Durley Rocks, which are less than half a mile out near the sewer buoy. Anglers go for the plaice and dabs on the sandy ground near the rocks as well as taking wrasse from the rocks themselves. Drift-fishing for plaice throughout this area, from Bournemouth

Pier to Branksome, is fruitful. About half a mile immediately off Bournemouth Pier are more rocks (watch for those lobster-pot path finders) which yield good pollack.

Further offshore, large mackerel shoals build up in summer, which give the angler good feathering sport – and which also bring in the tope.

Further to the east of Bournemouth, the Southbourne Rough (see Chapter 4) provides good mixed fishing, and some larger boats – 16ft and over – reach this mark from Poole Harbour. The Southbourne Rough also attracts small boats out of Christchurch and Mudeford as they can nip across Christchurch Ledge under Hengistbury for good fishing. Hengistbury Head Groyne, when fished from a dinghy with live sandeel, peeler crab, slipper limpet or mackerel strip, can be deadly for bass. Christchurch Bay has many sandy areas where plaice, dabs and mainly sole are taken, and further east, off Milton-on-Sea, there is a patch of rocks about three quarters of a mile offshore where conger, dogfish and pout come up well.

10 Boat Fishing in the Solent

The Solent is one of the busiest stretches of water along the south coast, its sheltered waters, good varied fishing and excessive tidal action drawing out hundreds of small angling boats – who must compete for water space with literally thousands of other boat users. The Solent divides the mainland of Hampshire from the Isle of Wight and is not quite five miles wide at its widest point, yet it is used by massive tankers loading and unloading at the Esso oil refinery at Fawley in Southampton Water, international liners and container ships using the Southampton Docks Ocean Terminal, cross-Channel ferries using the same port, passenger and car ferries linking the mainland with the Island, hovercraft and hydrofoil services doing the same, and in the summer season becomes a playground for the massive international yachting fleets centring on Cowes, Isle of Wight, and including the Hamble River.

Golden rule number one when fishing in the Solent is never to anchor in the deep-water channels; rule number two is always to keep a sharp look-out for trouble. Yacht racing fleets are busy from Gosport, Lee-on-Solent, Hill Head, Weston, also the Beaulieu and Lymington Rivers on the mainland, and Yarmouth, Cowes, Wootten and Ryde on the north Island shore, not to mention water skiers, even parascenders, and the Royal Navy which often turns up in the eastern Solent.

The greatest single factor governing fishing in the Solent is its tidal pattern, which has a double high tide each day. The West Solent is notorious for its raging tides, and when tide and wind oppose each other a confused and vicious sea results. An example of the power of the West Solent tide came in 1975 when a party of nine anglers out of Lymington were swept onto a buoy off Yarmouth. Their boat was held against the buoy by the tide until it went down – and only by good luck and the prompt action of other boats on the spot were all nine saved. Elsewhere in the Solent, the tidal streams are quite complex with some straight 12-hour cycles (the tide taking 7 hours to make to a high tide and 5 to fall to low tide) while in other spots it has double highs immediately following each other. Local knowledge is of prime importance in finding out what the tide will do next.

For fishing purposes I have divided the Solent into the West Solent, Southampton Water and the East Solent. At the entrance to the western extremity are the Shingles Banks which lie south-west of Hurst Spit and Hurst Castle and which are notorious for their tides – and famous for their bass. The Shingles are no place for the inexperienced in small boats. Under the guidance of locals they can be trolled for bass which are numerous and big. So too are the overfalls, with swirling cresting seas thrown up by raging tides sweeping the shallow water. The tope which are taken to the east of the Shingles towards the Needles, can also be taken in the channel between the Shingles and Hurst Spit. The centre of the channel through the West Solent is where the tide races, and where the larger ships run, and is avoided by small-boat anglers, for whom the best fishing is along the north-western Island shore and the south-west New Forest mainland shore.

One of the favourite small-boat marks out of Yarmouth is Black Rock, a mixed fishing area producing congers, the never-failing pout and dogfish, and – less often – pollack. It is one of the marks particularly susceptible to nasty sea conditions when the wind is against the tide. Straight off Yarmouth Harbour, thornbacks are taken when the neap tides permit fishing at all, and the skate frequent Hamstead Ledge guarding the western entrance to Newtown Harbour. This Ledge, about half a mile long, also yields congers (and more of those pout). From Newtown through the West Solent to Cowes, bass are taken in good numbers by trolling, with summer mackerel shoals adding sport.

On the western mainland side, good mixed fishing is to be had off Lymington with skate and conger – the latter especially round the sewer outlets – also dogfish and pout. Moving further into the West Solent, some excellent tope sport is found, together with good numbers of bass. The tope fishing runs from Lymington as far as the Beaulieu River and in some cases tope are taken as far north as Calshot. Off the Calshot Lightship there is a return of mixed fishing, with congers to be had (and more pout). Tope tackle employed in the West Solent enables the maximum use to be made of the tide in working the bait. A running leger is used to a wire trace, to guard against the tope fraying the trace with its rough skin.

Calshot is one spot where small-boat owners can suffer nightmares watching out for liners and tankers, ferries and yachts. Everything using Southampton Water comes past Calshot. It is a pity because the mixed fishing is generally good, with congers and skate – nearly all thornback – dogfish and pout, and a few whiting and cod in winter.

Calshot guards Southampton Water, a six-mile stretch of sheltered water, just over half of which can be fished and which basically produces flounders and bass. Along its western shore lie the tanker jetties and oil storage tanks of Fawley, which preclude fishing in that area, but further up Southampton Water is Hythe Bay, the first of the good flounder marks. In the upper reaches, the baited spoon method is very effective. Higher still, off Marchwood Power Station in the city itself, the warm water brings the bass in. Boat anglers are more fortunate with regard to fishing grounds on the eastern shore of Southampton Water, with the whole stretch from the Docks, past Weston Shore and Netley to the River Hamble yielding flounders, and a few bass. Off the mouth of the River Hamble – almost opposite the mixed fishing area of Calshot – is another good mixed fishing ground, around the Greenland Buoy.

East of the River Hamble mouth, back in the Solent proper, there is a tremendous variety of fishing, and many dozens of boats chase it from the mainland and north Isle of Wight shores. At Hill Head, boat anglers take good bass catches, and from the area immediately off Titchfield Haven I had reported to me catches of several sea trout and one salmon. Hill Head is noted for its richness in bait supplies. Off the sea wall to the west of Titchfield Haven are ragworm grounds – with some excellent king rag areas on the furthest extremities of low water during springs – and to the east, nearer Monkey Hill, are lugworm grounds.

Further east at Lee-on-Solent are marks which fished tremendously well during the 1950s and 1960s and which still

(*above*) Eastbourne, Sussex: the extreme western end of Eastbourne promenade looking beyond the fir trees to the clifflands of Beachy Head; (*below*) Mudeford Harbour (Dorset-Hampshire border): the view from Mudeford Quay looking across at the sand spit with the breakers in the harbour mouth in the background

Portland Bill, Dorset: along the eastern edge of Portland Bill are the ledges formed by the quarrying, ledges which afford platforms for anglers – but take great care with those breakers

provide rich mixed fishing. Any boat travelling about a mile offshore in the 'good old days' used to return with several cod on board in the winter, and whiting could be taken three at a time on old brass paternosters. Nowadays, the winter fishing is quieter, though a few cod come in every year from around the Browndown Ranges Danger Buoy and the East Brambles. In the summer months, these marks produce good thornback ray and bass catches together with dogfish, pout and the occasional smoothhound.

One favourite bait for the smoothhounds are hermit crabs – which abound off Lee, and which feed avidly on large squid baits during evening trips. Closer to the shore, the slipway off the Fleet Air Arm base at HMS *Daedalus*, Lee-on-Solent produces sole and bass – two local experts, Dave Elbourn and Gordon Wilkins, once taking five specimen sole in one trip on locally dug ragworm.

A few hundred yards to the east on the site where Lee Pier once stood, there still remains a good bass mark among the wreckage of the pier. Lee Pier – which suffered a fire many years ago, and which was blown up during World War II to ensure that invading Germans could not use it, always provided good bass fishing. Anglers drift-lined live sandeel on lead-shot-weighted lines under the pier where big bass to 8lb lurked. The sport was in trying to entice the bass away from the piles once they were hooked. One unusual aspect of this fishing was that the sandeels were locally *dug*. The demolition of Lee Pier – under which salvage divers later found enormous conger eels, big bass and plenty of lobsters – and later of Lee Tower robbed Solent anglers of two good landmarks for taking fixes. A bus terminal now stands where the Tower once stood, and directly beneath this, and close in to the beach, bass can still be caught – though not such big fish.

Off the Army rifle ranges at Browndown Military Camp is a sharp deep hole which produces congers, skate, dogfish, pout and whiting, and cod in winter. At one time dabs and flounders could be taken from most areas off Lee but their absence nowadays, together with the general decrease in catches off Lee, bears testimony to the battering the area has taken from commercial fishermen. Oyster dredgers have cleared an oyster bed off Lee – with as many as 22 boats seen working through the area at once – and trawlers also work over the mud flats. Completing the versatility of this area are the occasional unusual visitors – like the turbot – one 10lb fish, which I took came not 200yd from the beach – allis shad, twaite shad and brill.

In the summer, mackerel shoals work through the Solent with a tendency during latter years for bass to get mixed with them. One adaptation of feathering for mackerel which had the desired effect of picking up the bass, too, was to put a small red-gill in place of the bottom feather, or even trail it beneath the weight. It seemed that the bass were shoaling beneath the mackerel, and often the rig took a string of mackerel with a bass on the red-gill.

At the extreme eastern end of the Solent on the northern mainland shore is Stokes Bay, Gosport, a good general area for mixed fishing. Big bass are taken there in summer, cod in winter, and big tope and conger have been landed from dinghies, again less than a mile from the shore. One favourite mark is Stokes Bay Wreck buoy, about half a mile offshore. Conger are taken by anglers lucky enough to anchor over the several pieces of wreck that exist in the area. An echo-sounder is invaluable in finding them. You are more likely to pick up 'grand-dad'-size pout that abound round the wreck pieces. Gilkicker Point marks the eastern end of the Solent, and this too draws anglers after cod and whiting in winter, and bass in summer. It is another place to beware of a confused sea, as it is a meeting point for two tidal systems – out of Portsmouth Harbour from the east and the Solent from the west.

In addition to the tides, Gilkicker has some very deep water not far out from the point. One favourite mark for conger is a sudden drop in depth from about 8 fathoms to 12 fathoms – again a mark reserved for the angler armed with an echo-sounder – and further out is a larger area of water up to 15 fathoms deep. A few hundred yards west of Gilkicker Point are the remains of the derelict Stokes Bay pier. The pierhead remains crumbling into the sea, while the pier itself has been dismantled and removed. It provides a mark for small dinghies from which pout and small pollack are taken, together with small bass.

Throughout the area from Hill Head to Stokes Bay there are numerous launching sites for small boats. At Hill Head, there is Titchfield Haven itself with car-parking space to the west. One problem is that boats cannot be launched at dead low tide. They can be launched at the HMS *Daedalus* slipway, at a small slipway leading from the Council car park on Lee clifflands to the east of where the Tower stood, and from the two slipways at Elmore. The 1975 wooden slipway built for use by Elmore Angling Club was quickly wrecked by gales but has been repaired and is usable again. One hundred yards to the west is the concrete slipway – used mainly by the local sailing club – which is open to the public. It is extremely steep. At Stokes Bay boats can be launched all along the gently shelving beach, with the best facilities at the eastern end of the bay near the sailing and angling club premises. A new slipway came into use in conjunction with the Gosport and District Angling Club in 1979.

A series of mudbanks run through the central and eastern Solent from the Brambles Bank in the west to the Stourbridge Shoal in the east. The Brambles, centrally situated off Calshot, Hill Head, Lee and Cowes, is buoyed by four buoys – the East Brambles, West Brambles, South Brambles and Hill Head buoy. Next bank to the east is the Ryde Middle Bank – which is not off Ryde, but rather between Cowes and Wootton. It is buoyed by five buoys – the North, North East, South East, South and West Ryde Middles. Nearer the Island shore and running east to Wootton is the Peel Bank – with a single buoy of that name – and off Wootton itself is the Mother Bank – similarly buoyed. The best mixed fishing is found by anglers who anchor on the edges of the banks and fish down the sides. Good thornback catches are made from the banks from April to October, together with bass and dogfish.

Watch out for the Brambles Bank – literally. On the biggest spring tides of the year it dries out despite being in the centre of the Solent – probably as far from the land as you can get. I have played cricket on the Brambles on one such tide. Another word of warning when fishing this section of the Solent – the deep-water channel is literally only a few feet wider than the liners and heavy tankers that use it. They cannot alter course to miss you, so the responsibility lies with you in keeping clear of them.

Finally there remains the section of the Solent along the northern coast of the Island from Ryde to Cowes. The easternmost mark around the Stourbridge Shoal to the north-east of Ryde Pier is noted for big tope, and less often big congers. The ubiquitous pout frequent both the Mother and Ryde Middle

Banks and fishing in the strongest tide run can sometimes produce decent-size pout above the 1lb mark. Dogfish also feed during the full race of tide. From Ryde to Wootton, boats working the inshore mudflats take good catches of plaice and flounder from April to November, many of the best results coming from float fishing from a drifting boat. This is capitalising on the basic requirement when flatfish hunting – that you must keep the bait on the move. Locals, who have flatfishing off to a fine art here, can drift with the tide, sit through a slack and drift back to the starting point on the returning tide, taking fish in both directions. Assisting the boat anglers along this shore is the natural shelter provided by the Island. As the prevailing winds are from the south-west, this shore is more often than not in the lee of the land.

Good plaice fishing extends further west into Osborne Bay with the picturesque Kings Quay being a good mark. Here, also, bass are taken in good numbers by anglers trolling, and mackerel shoals often build up – especially during long summer evenings. The Osborne Bay area is another particularly busy hotch-potch of boats in summer, being so close to Cowes Harbour. One angler who has spent years studying the techniques of trolling for bass, and who has found Osborne Bay a particularly good hot spot, is Steve Gathergood. His experience has taught him precise combinations of time of day, state of tide, speed of shoals, depth of shoals, heat, wind and which tackle to produce his big bass catches, but his general findings are useful pointers to boat anglers throughout the Solent chasing the summer bass.

One way to locate feeding bass shoals is to watch the birds carefully. Any boat angler knows that wheeling, diving, swooping gulls spell fish – but not many can tell a mackerel shoal from a bass shoal by watching the birds. Experience shows that if the birds are working continuously low over the surface they are working a mackerel shoal, as the mackerel keep the whitebait (on which the birds are feeding) constantly in a shoal. If the birds work on the surface – and suddenly climb and circle for a few minutes and then dive and work again – they are over bass. The bass disperse the whitebait as they devour them, and then spend time getting another shoal lined up before attacking and again dispersing them. While the bass line up the next target shoal, the birds climb, circle and watch for the new action.

Consequently one piece of equipment for a bass-trolling enthusiast should be binoculars to spot the birds.

In the height of summer, the bass fanatic must be prepared to go afloat around 3am and be at sea in the Solent waiting for the first shoals to move as dawn breaks. Much of the best bass trolling comes at the two extremes of the day – dawn and dusk. The method is to motor uptide of the shoal – sometimes allowing the tide to do the work, sometimes the wind; you cast the lure – and there is an enormous field for experiment here – and retrieve. You need a high-ratio fast-retrieve fixed-spool reel ideally, and the lure can be retrieved at varying depths and speeds. The whole secret is the combination of depth, speed, action and positioning of casting that brings the top results. Many of the shoals of bass work from Stokes Bay, through the central Solent, through the Osborne Bay hot spot and down into the West Solent.

One final word of warning about the water traffic in the Solent – watch out for the washes from large liners and ships. In the Solent, washes tend to be steeper and fiercer than in the open Channel because it is narrow and confined. Not only must the wash be watched carefully if you are fishing near a passing ship, but a moment of danger can arrive if you launch or return to a beach as a wash hits. I have seen many boats swamped as a result of such unfortunate timing. There are precautions you can take. When at sea, if a wash appears to be steep and about to endanger you, swing your boat round on its anchor rope so that you are bow-on to the wash, and you will ride it out happily. One of the steepest washes of all encountered in the Solent are those from submarines. If you are about to land on a beach and a wash is following you in, stand off the beach for a minute or two until it has hit the shore. Also remember that there should be two washes for every ship – first the bow wave hitting the beach and then the wash from the screws.

11 Boat Fishing South of the Isle of Wight

While the northern coast of the Isle of Wight facing the Solent (Chapter 10) supports an enormous quantity of small-boat angling, the south-western shores facing the English Channel are bleak and just about devoid of small boats. Between the Needles and St Catherine's Point there are no harbours from which to launch a boat, and with the south-westerly winds prevailing the area is constantly rough, with heavy seas pounding the south-western beaches. Some boats out of Yarmouth fish round the Needles in Freshwater Bay and Compton Bay, where there are large congers, skate, pout and dogfish in the rocky patches dotted around the area. Most boats that do any fishing between the Needles and St Catherine's are the shark boats patrolling the deeps a few miles south of St Catherine's itself. These boats also hit large tope.

Between St Catherine's and Ventnor almost on the point of Dunnose, which is the south-eastern corner of the Island, fierce tides and rock patches, coupled with the prevailing south-westerly wind, make this another area not often fished by small boats, but Dunnose Head is becoming an increasingly popular venue – especially with boats travelling from the mainland. Boats from the Eastern Solent, Portsmouth and Langstone Harbours, and Bembridge and the eastern seaboard of the Island travel south to Dunnose whenever a neap tide coincides with calm weather. Those two requirements are fundamental, for Dunnose Head boasts some fierce tides – impossible to fish on springs, and only comfortably possible on neaps with the use of wire (see Chapter 3). Although the entire area of Dunnose is rocky, there are rock plateaux which are less productive than sharp, broken rock. Most boats taking the trouble to motor so far to fish the area are equipped with an echo-sounder to ensure they can pick up the deep holes in the rock, and the broken areas of ground.

Basically there are two favourite marks off Dunnose. Close in to the east of Ventnor, there is a deep rocky trench – but it suffers the worst tides of all and is practically unfishable all the time. Anglers who can fish it with wire catch very large congers and huss. Outside this deep trench is a further bank of rocky ground topped by large rocks which make the water quite shallow, and outside this area is a huge drop into a hole more than 35 fathoms deep. This is the main Dunnose mark. It has slightly fewer fierce tides, and produces regular catches of congers, huss, dogfish, black bream, occasional pollack, and even cod in winter. Congers have a great deal of rock to wrap their tails round on these marks, and anglers hooking congers here must get them away from the seabed fast or risk having the conger – which is the only fish that can move backwards as effectively as forwards – drag his gear back into the rocks in a few seconds.

Further inshore, off Luccombe Village, lies a rocky ledge which provides conger, pollack and huss sport for smaller boats out of Ventnor, Shanklin and Sandown. Bass are taken between this ledge and Horse Ledge which lies further east towards Shanklin. Off Shanklin itself there are two main quarries. In summer, black bream move into the rocky area immediately offshore from Shanklin Pier and about half a mile out, while tope anglers find sport in the same area south of Sandown Bay. Sandown Bay itself has isolated rock patches and a few old wrecks about three miles from shore. There are some huge conger in both areas, and one 14ft dinghy that travelled all the way from Gosport a few years ago went back with a 53lb conger from Sandown Bay. The Bay is subject not only to strong tides, but eddying tides. Between the rocky patches there are sandy stretches which produce rays, and a few cod are taken in winter.

Sandown Bay is flanked to the north by Culver Cliffs, off which anglers troll live sandeels for bass. The true art of this method at this location is understanding and using the tide. A strong tide boils and swirls on the surface offshore from these cliffs. The best fishing of all of this section of coastline comes from the area between Culver Cliff and the Foreland at Bembridge. Offshore at Culver Cliff and stretching north towards Bembridge are the Princessa Shoals, and off Bembridge itself is the Bembridge Ledge. The Princessa Shoals are spread over a large area to the east and offshore from the Princessa Buoy, and as far north almost as the southern extremes of Bembridge Ledge.

A lesson about fishing near buoys is well illustrated with the Princessa Shoal Buoy. Many anglers fishing a mark, fish near the buoy itself (for example, the Dean Tail Buoy when the cod season is in full swing often attracts up to 60 boats). The more successful angler does not use the buoy as the marker. Rather he finds out what the buoy is marking and fishes that. The Princessa Shoal Buoy marks the shoal, but the best fishing is to be had maybe a mile east of it, and other marks north-east are good. The area – broken patches of rock with sand and rough ground interspersed – is tremendous black bream ground in summer. During May and June huge bream shoals build up over the Shoals, and one useful method is to move occasionally if the bream stop coming. Small distances of 20 or 30yd can put you on rocks where the bream are feeding. Absolute precision rock location by an echo-sounder is invaluable in chasing the bream on the Shoals. At other times of the year the Shoals produce good mixed fishing – with skate, rays, dogfish and conger throughout the year and big cod in winter.

Bembridge Ledge is a rocky ledge extending for about a mile east of the Bembridge Foreland which is the easternmost tip of the Island. The eastern extremity of the ledge is marked by the Bembridge Ledge Buoy. Strong tides race over the rocks, which are very broken, which have areas of very shallow water over them, and which can be dangerous with occasional east or north-east winds blowing on to them. Small black bream, conger, huss, pollack, wrasse and pout are taken over the ledge with cod being taken in winter. One remarkable catch made off the Ledge came in November 1975 when Bembridge charter skipper and angling expert Robin Horspool took ten 20lb cod in three hours.

The best mark is again not near the Buoy itself but in this case to the south-west where the rocks of the ledge cease. This is one point where anglers can use the lobster-pot marker buoys as an indication of where the rocks lie. Once again, an echo-sounder is invaluable for this area. The same lobster-pot buoys which are useful for anyone fishing the ledge are also a menace for boats travelling through the area to the grounds further south. When motoring through this area, keep a sharp look-out for pot buoys all the way from Bembridge to the Princessa Buoy. There are others, less numerous, on rocky patches in Sandown Bay.

From Bembridge to Seaview, and especially around St Helen's Fort between the two, is an area in the grips of one of the worst menaces threatening sea angling in the area – the growth of *sargassum muticum*, colloquially known as Japanese seaweed. It was first identified in February 1973 and has been multiplying at an alarming rate. During the summer, the weed grows fastest, and strands attached to the seabed regularly attain lengths of 25ft. At its thickest points the weed clogs propellers, and boats cannot drive through it. Scientists have spent many thousands of pounds on research on the weed, and trying to find ways of killing it, all without success.

When it was first discovered, there were working parties on the Island which gathered the weed and burned it. It grew faster than they could destroy it, and it is now out of control. It has crossed the Solent and is well established in the upper reaches of Portsmouth Harbour, and in Langstone Harbour. In 1976 one fleet of small outboard dinghies returning to their moorings at Port's Creek after a fishing trip all became ensnared in the weed, which tangled round the props and had to be cut and hacked away. It is known to be spreading along the northern coast of the Island, and scientists have discovered it also in the west country. About the only defence against the weed seems to be extremely cold temperatures – during the winter months it stops growing. But each winter is no more than a respite before the weed continues to flourish each successive summer.

The Ecology Department of Portsmouth Polytechnic in conjunction with the Marine Laboratory at Hayling Island has spearheaded the research work. Scientists there see potential 'doomwatch' results if there is no control of the weed. They have recorded it growing up to four centimetres a day, and have known it survive temperatures as low as $1\frac{1}{2}°C$ in pools in Bembridge Harbour, and as high as $24°C$ when the summer sun has heated the same pools. The scientists have now conceded that the weed is too well established for them to wipe it out and are concentrating on confining it. Sea anglers can positively help them in this work. Those scientists I talked to are anxious to hear from all anglers – especially those away from the Solent – who find strands of the weed floating, or worse still growing. Findings of the weed should be reported to them at the Biology Department, Portsmouth Polytechnic or the Marine Laboratories, Hayling Island. In this way you will be helping to prevent this menace from spreading.

Along the stretch of inshore water between Nettlestone Point at Seaview and Ryde Pier, plaice fishing is predominant, especially over Ryde Sands. This is an area of shallow water – the area immediately east of the Pier drying out over an enormous distance at low tide.

12 Boat Fishing inside the Nab

Some of the most concentrated small-boat and dinghy fishing in southern England abounds in the Spithead area and the area inside the Nab Tower. In the stretch of sea bounded by Haslar Sea Wall and the mainland of Portsmouth and Hayling Island in the north, the Selsey Bill peninsula to the east, and the Ryde to Bembridge north-east corner of the Island there are dozens of marks to attract all aspects of small-boat fishing – from conger and skate spots to flatfish grounds. Small boats flood into this area from the mainland of Gosport and Lee (especially with the modern trend for slightly larger boats with powerful engines), from Portsmouth Harbour, Langstone Harbour, Chichester Harbour, from the Witterings and Selsey, and from the Isle of Wight ports of Ryde, Seaview, St Helen's and Bembridge.

Although it is not as confined as the Solent, the area still provides problems of congestion, with much naval activity, and a large number of ocean-going yachts crossroading through the area either along the coast towards the Solent and Cowes, or setting off or returning from Cherbourg and Northern France. Liners, ferries, coasters and tankers move through the area, with more recent additional traffic from the enormous container ships visiting Southampton.

On top of this, the number of fishing boats is constantly increasing. Several times during the flood of cod catches during the winters of 1977–79, individual marks – such as Dean Tail – were surrounded by up to 120 small boats. The westernmost mark in the area are the Mining Grounds about two miles off Ryde, midway between Ryde and Gilkicker, almost into the eastern end of the Solent. The immediate attraction of this spot is that big fish can be taken over the rough ground which is well strewn with debris. There are often anxious moments with snagging anchors in this area, and anchor tripping is essential. General fishing can provide a steady stream of big pout, interspersed with skate – especially big thornback – congers, tope and even sting ray.

Quite often, visiting anglers fish the Mining Grounds with light tackle, happily taking pout, and get smashed by these big fish. It is a mark where you should always be prepared to encounter good fish. Even charter boats are tempted into this mark if the weather cuts out the deep-water marks. Periodically, the Royal Navy explodes mines in the area, so if there appears to be any warship activity in the Mining Grounds, steer clear. You will be warned away from the area when mining is in progress. In summer, the mark produces a black bream potential if the favoured grounds further east are inaccessible because of bad weather. Although numerous, the bream here are small on average.

Across Spithead, dinghy fishing takes place along the southern coast of Portsmouth with flatfish being taken off Southsea, and the area off South Parade Pier producing codling in winter. The next major dinghy mark off Southsea is The Blocks – which are prolific for bass. Plaice and pollack are also taken in lesser numbers. The Blocks are a relic from the days of World War II when it was decided to form an anti-submarine sea defence for Spithead and ultimately Portsmouth Harbour by sinking huge concrete blocks, supporting a pile sticking up from the seabed. They stretch from the shore at Southsea almost opposite Lumps Fort east of South Parade Pier, to Horse Sands Fort. They are continued on the Isle of Wight side from No Man's Fort to Seaview Point. Since the war many of the piles have been removed; certainly all the iron stakes on the inshore three quarters of the blocks are gone. Nearer Horse Sands Fort several of the irons still remain, while on the Island side, they have all been removed. But the concrete blocks are still present and they represent a major hazard to navigation and must be approached carefully.

There are two gaps through the Southsea blocks. About 200yd offshore, a narrow gap through the blocks is marked by two poles, while further out is the main gap, marked by a dolphin and a buoy. Local dinghy anglers have perfected a killing method of fishing for the bass that run to a good size on the blocks. It entails anchoring the dinghy well clear of the blocks, and allowing the craft to drop back on the anchor rope until it is positioned just up-tide of the target area. The tackle used is light, allowing a live sandeel to be worked down the tide over and between the blocks. The bass take close to the blocks themselves and many are lost once the angler lets the bass retreat into its lair in the concrete.

Further east along the Southsea beach lies the West Winner bank, off the entrance to Langstone Harbour. It is an excellent bank for plaice, flounders and bass with silver eels sometimes making themselves unwelcome. Plaice congregate over the West Winner in early April prior to spreading out along the beaches. While the bank attracts anglers out of Portsmouth and Langstone Harbours, others travel from as far as Gosport in the west and the Witterings in the east for the flatfishing here. Baited spoon is particularly effective. Allow the bait to settle on the bank; gently raise the rod from time to time to flutter the spoon and attract the plaice. A Gosport specialist, Steve Mills, and some Gosport and District Angling Club colleagues took more than 100 plaice from the bank in four trips in April 1976. In two hours' fishing I took five to 2lb 9ozs.

Across the Langstone Harbour entrance the East Winner bank provides the same excellent plaice fishing. It is a longer sandbank, stretching almost two miles out to sea, and can be clearly seen at low water. It dries out along most of its length, and even a moderate wind will mark the bank with a line of crashing breakers. Some dogfish and occasional skate are taken from its outer end, and boats fishing the Langstone Fairway – between the two banks – achieve good mixed fishing results. Best fishing comes from just inside the Fairway Buoy – although anglers must be sure to keep the channel clear. In summer the area provides good mackerel spinning, black bream, pout and plaice fishing, with a few codling in October and November, and whiting in winter.

Further south-east into Hayling Bay are Church Rocks, which provide mixed fishing likely to include the three main species of ray – thornback, small-eyed and spotted – and even cod in winter. Several clear landmarks line up to give a decent fix for Church Rocks. Line up the tower on Gilkicker Point with Spit Sand Fort and the Eastney Pumping Station chimney with the Milton Tower Block. While plaice, dabs, pout and dogfish are taken regularly, always be prepared for the bigger species to turn up. Church Rocks are the first of numerous marks in this area where rays are taken. Most commonly caught are the thornbacks, and although the record thornback stands at 38lb any fish over 12lb is a good ray. In the Spithead area they run from about the 7lb to the 18lb mark. Small-eyed rays or painted rays are much smaller than thornbacks, while the spotted or homelyn ray is the smallest of all the rays commonly found in this area. One useful attribute of these two smaller rays is that they sometimes feed on ragworm being offered for plaice and dabs in the Church Rocks area.

Further east, outside the entrance to Chichester Harbour, bass is the favourite quarry, with live sandeels or artificial lures being trolled and drift-lined. On the east side outside the entrance, tope run in good numbers, with sliding leger to a wire trace the main method of fishing for them. In some cases the tope are taken almost as far as the East Winner Bank. Further off, into Bracklesham Bay, the area between Chichester Harbour entrance and Selsey Bill consists of a host of rough patches of ground, all attracting excellent mixed fishing.

One such mark is south of the 'Targets' – two poles marking the wreck of a Mulberry which lies in a north–south plane. The Mulberry Harbours were enormous concrete structures built during World War II as sections of floating harbour walls to be towed to the northern coast of France to provide shelter for the invading Allied forces after D-Day. The wreck of one of these structures is clearly visible in Langstone Harbour while another wrecked Mulberry lies in Bracklesham Bay. By lining up the two marker poles and travelling due south along that line for about 20 minutes, the angler comes to a mark which produces excellent bass in summer – fish up to 12lb were taken in 1976 – and cod in winter.

Bracklesham's mixed fishing consists of dogfish, pout, skate, conger and huss, with the seasonal bonuses of black bream in summer and cod in winter. Additionally, there are occasional visitors like monkfish – taken to 56lb in recent years – and the odd angler fish.

Moving back towards Spithead and the west further offshore, there lie some top mixed fishing grounds which provide a happy medium of providing small-boat owners with big fish opportunities, of the calibre that attracts charter skippers. The favourite of these marks, about four miles south of the entrance to Langstone Harbour, is Dean Tail. This is one mark likely to attract up to 100 boats on winter weekends when the cod are in. Cod run big off this mark – with several to 28lb caught in the winter of 1976, and a flood of even bigger fish taken in the boom year of 1979.

Throughout the late summer, autumn and winter of 1976 the Dean Tail mark was subject to the same welcome arrival of surprising numbers of large pollack as were the grounds off the Needles. Some of the deep-water wrecks had provided big pollack earlier in the year, with a 17lb 3oz fish reported to me by Dave Coombs, skipper of the *Southern Cross*. But as the year progressed, it became clear that pollack were coming in on bottom-fishing tackle intended for skate and cod. One former Langstone Harbour skipper, Ged Pearce, who now runs *Lucky Strike* out of Brighton Marina, showed initiative when one of his party hit a pollack. By feathering with baited cod feathers he was rewarded with another six. Fish between 7lb and 10lb were coming in regularly, when Dean Tail took its fair share up to 14lb. For other parts of the coast – mainly the west country – these fish are not spectacular, but they became the major talking point of this area.

In one way they masked the bad news of the 1976 winter season – that the cod had slumped a little despite an early mad flood in November. Charter skippers' carefully kept logs showed that ten years earlier nearly every trip produced cod (with catches of 11 cod at a time on record), whereas during 1976 the boats struggled to take a dozen during the whole season. The only consolation, as always in this area, was that without fail the cod brought in were big. By the late 1970s the position had improved again with 1979 being a fabulous cod winter in this area. Marks to the east and north-east of the Dean Tail buoy itself are favourite over ground which is undulating with gullies. Heading towards Portsmouth Harbour from Dean Tail, the Dean Elbow buoy marks ground which provides more good mixed fishing – especially for tope in summer, and skate for much of the year. The buoy itself lies about two miles south of the Horse Sands Fort, and the best fishing is to be had to the north and north-east of the buoy. The large area of mixed fishing spreads inshore further over the Dean Sands where plaice and dabs are caught together with pout, dogfish, skate, and cod in winter.

Dean Sands is another area, like Church Rocks, which falls conveniently at the intersection of clearly visible landmarks on most days. One fix is gained by lining up No Man's Fort and Horse Sands Fort and the cross-bearing comes by lining up Spit Sands Fort (the one nearest Portsmouth Harbour) in the gap between the dolphins in the Blocks anti-submarine defences. Between Dean Sands and Dean Tail is a heavily fished mark called the 25-minute mark – which also yields mixed fishing, including occasional big fish – mostly skate. Although fishing further west round the Forts themselves produces dabs and plaice – with bream and bass in the summer – they each have a potential for big fish lying nearby. Off the Horse Sands Fort it is in the form of a wreck buoy lying about half a mile off, which has given conger, while a deep-water mark to the south of No Man's Land Fort is a favourite ray mark.

One word of warning to anglers venturing to fish around Spit Sands Fort. Directly south of the Fort is the site of the wreck of the *Mary Rose* – a Tudor battleship which sank in 1545, and which is currently the subject of a major archaeological expedition which eventually hopes to raise the wooden vessel. The site is protected by the Crown and is clearly marked and buoyed. The wreck itself lies buried under the seabed, and diving usually continues on it throughout the summer. An interesting point for anglers concerns the fish which congregate around the divers. Expedition leader and discoverer of the wreck, Mr Alexander McKee, told me of the resident thornback that sits in the bottom of the trench dug in order to reach the ship, and of the vast numbers of pout that have to be literally knocked out of the way by the divers before they can start work.

Nearer the entrance to Portsmouth Harbour, bass can be taken by trolling or by drifting live sandeels, but this entrance is the worst of the three (Portsmouth, Langstone and Chichester) for congestion. Royal Navy warships, Isle of Wight passenger ferries and car ferries, and the new cross-Channel ferries are all large vessels with no room whatsoever to manoeuvre in the narrow entrance. The Isle of Wight – Clarence Pier hovercraft is another constant visitor, and the whole area is sprinkled with

The author with a 22lb cod taken on squid in the Nab Tower grounds on a day when a 38lb giant was also landed

(*above*) Poole Harbour, Dorset: some of the charter fleet tucked away in the upper reaches of the harbour opposite Poole power station; (*below*) another fine cod about to be gaffed in the Nab Tower grounds and lifted aboard one of the Langstone Harbour charter-boats

yachts from the huge Camper and Nicholson marina inside the Harbour.

During the mid 1960s the area between Portsmouth Harbour mouth and Spit Sands Fort – over Spit Sands – was a favourite hot bed for plaice and dabs, and catches of 100 or more a day were taken regularly. Since that time – especially as the area is immediately accessible from the harbour mouth – the fishing has become poorer. As soon as the flatfish arrive and mass on the sands the trawlers are in. Anglers who compete with and beat the trawlers can still take plaice.

13 Boat Fishing:
Selsey to Brighton

Small-boat fishing in West Sussex, from Selsey Bill to Black Rock off Brighton, is blessed by revelling in both summer and winter opportunities. Some of the finest black bream fishing along the south coast is available to the small-boat owner in summer – especially from Littlehampton – while big tope add to the summer's excitement within the range of small boats. In winter, big cod run through the area. Providing a backcloth to the seasonal changes are the bass and flatfish catches which are excellent for much of the year.

First of the good bass marks are the rocky areas off Selsey Bill. While the rocks provide an excellent draw for fish, they can also be dangerous. A strong tide races off the Bill among the rocks and can cause steep confused seas. The rocks off the Bill are located simply by watching for the lobster-pot marker buoys. On no account should they be touched, but they give an excellent guide for fishing. Many of the best bass fall for red-gills trolled through the tide races (or sandeels, or spinners). In summer, these rocks attract big shoals of black bream. Thin strips of squid on long flowing traces are an effective method of taking them. Many anglers keep the bream on the feed by means of a ground-bait bag, either attached to the anchor rope near the anchor, or attached to a heavily weighted line. Most of the rocks off Selsey produce conger especially during evenings in late summer – July and August – and rays are taken from the sandy areas between the rock patches. Usually thornbacks are taken, but in 1976 there was an increase in the number of small-eyed rays. Further offshore, off Selsey, there are numerous packs of tope in summer and some huge fish – topping 50lb – have been caught.

In contrast, dinghies working close inshore on the eastern side of the Selsey Bill peninsula towards Pagham Harbour take good catches of plaice. Beyond Pagham Harbour, flatfish fishing continues close inshore as far as Bognor, where it improves. Bognor Regis offers good boat-launching facilities, and off its sandy inshore seabed all four main flatfish species can be taken. Small dinghies must be wary, off Bognor, of the Bognor Spit, which is visible as a curved reef of rocks at low tide, but which is covered after half tide. In places, however, there is as little as 2ft of water covering the reef. Fishing is excellent for bass – with the biggest fish falling to live prawn. This method sometimes produces pollack.

On the outside end of the reef, the congers can be taken on large mackerel baits – again with long summer evenings being favourite. The all-the-year-round attraction of Sussex is well illustrated off Bognor where there are rocky and rough patches about four miles out which provide excellent black bream fishing in summer (particularly May and June), good mixed fishing – dogfish, bull huss, skate and conger for most of the year, and cod and whiting in winter. One interesting feature of Bognor is that its tides are comparatively weak. A few miles away at Selsey tides are fierce, while off the resort they never run hard. One result is that many Bognor locals float fish for bream in summer over many of the rocky patches. The big tope which are a feature of the deeper water marks off Selsey run through the Bognor offshore areas.

Probably the best of West Sussex boat-fishing venues is Littlehampton – which is famous throughout Britain for its black bream catches in summer, and to a lesser degree its whiting fishing in winter. Littlehampton is the harbour where the River Arun meets the sea. Its stronger tides, and numerous rocky patches well offshore, make it better for larger boats than for small dinghies. Indeed, if there is a fair southerly wind blowing into the harbour, it can be downright dangerous trying to get out in a very small dinghy. Once outside, in summer, nearly every boat heads for the Kingsmere Rocks, situated 5½ miles south-east of Littlehampton. Ask a local for the best means of locating the mark and he will tell you to watch for the biggest single gathering of small and big boats on the horizon, and join them.

Black bream fishing begins really early off Littlehampton, with the first catches being made in April each year. During April, May and June they are in full cry, but later in the year, when the majority of the bream travel westwards along the south coast, only stragglers remain. Once again, ground-bait bags help enormously to keep the bream shoals on the feed. One successful match angler along the south coast, Ron Lambert of Portsmouth, swears by the effectiveness of boiled rice in the ground bait. While it keeps the bream feeding on whatever hook bait is being used, they are also enjoying the rice – as proven when he cut several open and found them well filled with rice. Careful bait presentation helps bream fishing. Chunks of whatever bait is being used – squid, mackerel, herring – are no good. The angler needs thin strips hooked at one end, so that the remaining tail works in the tide (in conjunction with a very long flowing trace) to imitate a small fish. These same rocky bream marks provide good mixed fishing with conger, skate and bull huss, small pollack, pout, and even cod in winter. One surprise in store for the bream angler can be the occasional meetings with congers or tope on bream tackle. Quite often congers will take a bream that has just taken a bait, or tope will take a bream on the way up. The alert angler – equipped to adapt his tackle – can switch to a wire trace and fish deliberately for tope or conger in these circumstances, using a bream fillet as bait.

Other bream marks off Littlehampton include the Ditches, which are another patch of rocks about a mile inside Kingsmere Rocks and much further to the west, and the marks around the Winter Knoll, which are no more than 1½ miles out from Littlehampton and which provide good mixed fishing in addition to bream catches in summer. Visiting anglers can nearly always assure themselves of bream catches by finding rock areas indicated by lobster-pot buoy markers. Packs of spur-dog range into these mixed fishing areas, and any boat angler lucky enough to run into them can enjoy spectacular sport. Throughout the area from Selsey through to Littlehampton there are mackerel shoals feeding all summer.

Between Littlehampton and Shoreham lies Worthing, the waters off which are mainly shallow, and which offer good flatfish grounds for anglers in boats. Plaice are probably the most prolific flatties, and they can be taken up to a mile out of Worthing. Further west between Littlehampton and Worthing lies Goring, which has rocky patches about a mile out which produce mixed fishing. The general trend of the area for good tope fishing is continued here.

On the eastern side of Worthing, at Lancing, there is good bass fishing, especially for the angler who obtains his own live sandeels in preference to trolling with red-gills. Bass fishing is another main attraction close inshore off Shoreham, but the strength of Shoreham is that it has fishing for miles out. Among its inshore marks, in addition to general flatfish hunting, and bass immediately off the harbour, are the Church Rocks. Close in to the west of Shoreham they yield black bream in summer. The sets of marks off the extreme eastern end of Shoreham provide pout and dogfish all the year round, plus all the mixed fishing possible – huss, skate, pollack and conger, with cod and whiting in winter. Between these marks and about 1½ miles off Shoreham is a wreck often fished by small boats. It holds pout and conger for most of the year – with bream shoals in summer, and whiting in winter. Outside the inshore wreck, at intervals stretching to about a maximum of seven miles out, are various rocky areas, all of which are good for mixed fishing, with the larger species, especially conger and tope, being taken from the outermost marks.

This section of coastline has its small-boat centre at Brighton which entices a large number of boat anglers with a varied range of species. Off Brighton there are a great number of rocks and rocky patches, all comparatively close inshore – and therefore well fished. They all produce pout, bream (in summer) some skate, a few congers, whiting and a few codling (in winter) and plaice and dabs in the areas of sand between the rock patches. Probably the best known of Brighton rocks (apart from the pink stuff with writing all through it) is Black Rock, situated at the extreme eastern end of the resort. It produces conger and cod (in winter) and mixed fishing throughout the area immediately out to sea for about a mile. The Black Rock itself yields bass. In summer, all the Brighton rock marks take good bream catches with one feature being that the bream stay from June right through to August and September. Outside the Black Rock area at the eastern end of Brighton is Measors Rock, which produces some big bull huss. For several years, Brighton held the British bull huss record with a fish of 21lb.

Between the two marks and further to the west off West Pier is Rock Tow – where in addition to the mixed fishing provided elsewhere, many good tope are taken. Quite often boat anglers take 40lb-plus tope off Brighton during summer and the early autumn months. One of the favourite marks for this rock-based mixed fishing at the Hove (western) end of Brighton is Loo Gate, which is further offshore than the other marks, and which yields larger species, especially conger, huss and tope. Further inshore at the Hove end are the more sandy areas which produce plaice, dabs and skate in the summer (mainly thornbacks) and whiting in winter. An exception is a mark off the Sussex County Hospital along towards Black Rock, which similarly produces flatfish and rays. The whole area is visited by mackerel shoals in summer – providing the best bait for the tope which run through the marks further offshore.

14 Boat Fishing: Newhaven to Rye

There is a natural break along the Sussex coastline between
Brighton and Newhaven, formed by high clifflands, but
Newhaven marks the resumption of boat fishing. Between
Newhaven and the Kent border, nearly 30 miles further east,
there are three main centres of small-boat fishing, at Newhaven
itself, Eastbourne and Hastings.

Newhaven, virtually at the mouth of the River Ouse, provides
launching facilities for small boats, which can enjoy the shelter of
the long breakwater at the harbour entrance. Most anglers know
of Newhaven for its very busy chartering trade (see Chapter 6)
but there are many fruitful inshore marks for small boats —
including the luxury of inshore wrecks to be fished. Newhaven
produces rich mixed fishing — pout, dogfish, huss, skate — plus
the summer additions of bream, pollack, plenty of good tope and
heavy shoals of mackerel, with whiting and cod in winter. Two
of the best-known marks off Newhaven are the Red Shrave and
the Dredger Dumping Grounds. The Red Shrave is a line of
rocks just over a mile offshore from the harbour breakwater
which give whiting and codling in winter (together with the
inevitable pout) and which have plaice and dabs in the sandy
areas lying around them. Nearly a mile further out is the
Dredger Dumping Grounds, which can be excellent for plaice
and dabs on its day. Sole are also taken over this general area —
with more whiting in winter. Worm baits are recommended
throughout this area. The inshore flatfish grounds continue to
the west along the coast between Peacehaven and Rottingdean,
where the whiting also fill in during winter.

For Newhaven's wrecks, most anglers will need to consult the
locals as the marks are spread from about four miles to ten miles
out from Newhaven. The charter boats go to the wrecks furthest

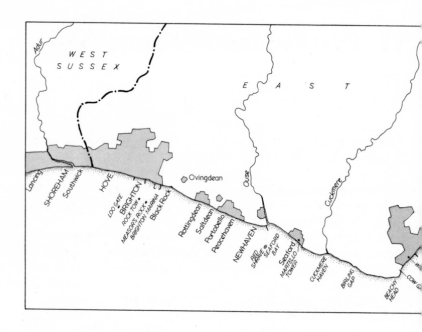

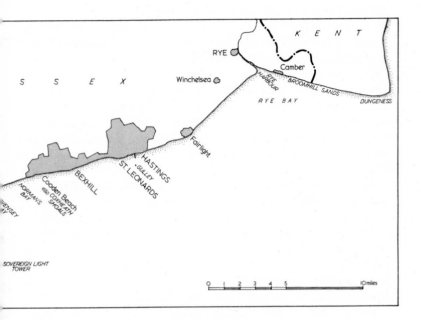

afield. There is a cluster of three or four wrecks about four miles out between Newhaven and Peacehaven, which yields good conger, pollack, black bream in summer and pout all the time. Many boats out of Newhaven turn east and fish the rich inshore marks off Seaford, the small town with a sea-wall promenade and launching facilities of its own for dinghies. It does face the prevailing south-westerly wind and anglers having to return to Seaford would be well warned to keep a wary eye on the weather. At the western end of Seaford, about 500yd out, in Tide Mills Bay, there is excellent sole and flounder fishing – provided the angler is prepared to experiment with bait. Razorfish, slipper limpet, white rag and red river rag are all as good if not better than lugworm at this spot.

At the other end of Seaford – between the Martello Tower and Splash Point, again about 500yd out – lies Town Rock which yields whiting and cod in winter and bass in summer. Here lugworm, squid and herring strip are the choice baits. Immediately offshore from the Martello Tower, about 1½ miles out, is a large rocky broken area which provides mixed fishing, with dogfish, huss, pout, some conger and skate. Squid and herring strip are the main baits for this area.

Further east of Seaford there is good mixed fishing towards Cuckmere Haven, and further west towards Beachy Head there is a favourite boat mark at Birling Gap – which sometimes even attracts the Newhaven charter boats. In summer Birling Gap provides rich bass sport for anglers trolling a sandeel, while in winter it yields cod.

Beachy Head itself is a fabulous bass fishing spot for those with a sound boat and either local knowledge or the assistance of a local boatman. Before going into the wealth of bass – and other – fishing off Beachy Head I must emphasise the dangers of fishing here in any kind of wind or with any bad forecast in the air. The strong tides off the Head whip the seas over the rocks into fierce overfalls and crashing white surf. But when conditions are right this area can be a real treat. Eastbourne fishing expert Brian Meades (who has fished for England and won numerous all-England open boat and beach matches) fishes Beachy Head regularly – and reckons that one day it will produce a bass to smash the British record. He and his colleagues out of Eastbourne who have fished for the bass, have still been smashed by huge fish they could not hold, even knowing what to expect and tackling up appropriately. The top bass mark here is the Beachy Head Ledge, approximately half a mile west of the lighthouse, fishing from May to July. The best method is trolling at low water actually into the broken water, using red-gills or other lures. As you can imagine, this calls for top-class boatmanship together with a sound knowledge of the tides off the Ledge and the effect of wind and seas. Sometimes, when it is flat calm with no wind, clear water and the tide is right, massive hauls of bass can be taken.

Two of the local clubs, Eastbourne Angling Association and, more recently, the Eastbourne Working Men's Club, have imposed a six-fish limit on their own members for the purpose of conservation, which is an excellent example to others. But bass are not the only fish available off Beachy Head. It is internationally famous for its tope.

The main tope grounds are to the west of the Ledge, straight off the lighthouse, and some huge catches of tope, running into hundreds of pounds, have been made. The rocks off Beachy Head are also home to a great variety of fish reached by bottom fishing – with conger, huss, skate, pout, and even cod and whiting in winter. Bottom fishing should be done on a small tide – and anglers would be well advised to carry a grapple or killick for anchoring. The seabed off here must be festooned with lost anchors.

One plaice and sole hot spot for local anglers immediately on the Eastbourne side of Beachy Head is the mark called the Goldmine. This is about 500yd out and 500yd west of the Sugar Loaf Rock at Hollywell. It is a small area of mud, sand and shingle, and the angler needs to sound the bottom with a heavy weight until he is sure he is on the mud and sand, before fishing. The best results come with lugworm bait after high water as the tide starts to ebb.

Round the corner from Beachy Head is Eastbourne, which is probably one of the very best small-boat fishing areas in the entire south, giving an enormous variety of fish from marks a few hundred yards offshore to spectacular catches up to ten miles out. In the past few years a quiet revolution has overtaken many of the private boats out of Eastbourne. They have become larger with more powerful engines and are beginning to venture further into the deep-water marks. Once again, this trend is being coupled in many cases with the use of echo-sounders, which have added a new dimension to boat fishing. One such pioneer of the new Eastbourne deep-water marks is Brian Meades, who has tried the fishing some five miles out from the Sovereign Light Tower which is itself about 5½ miles out from Eastbourne. The Tower has replaced the former Royal Sovereign Lightship, which no longer exists. These very deep water marks – some up to 37 fathoms – must be fished on a small tide and by pairs of boats for safety. They should not be attempted in bad weather, and at all times anglers must keep a wary eye open for shipping travelling through the Channel. Anglers should be equipped to deal with some really big fish. Already big congers, big rays, tope, good bull huss and 'grand-dad' pout have come from out of the deep.

For those anglers without an echo-sounder (which immediately shows the deep-water shelf dropping away) a simple time-run calculation should ensure success. If the angler times his run from Eastbourne to the Light Tower – and runs for the same period again due offshore, he should be in the deep. But for those with echo-sounders there is the additional perk of fishing new wrecks in the deep. Already these have produced good ling – almost unheard of in this part of the world – and summer wreck cod.

The area surrounding the Light Tower is another tremendous spot for small boats. Anglers must be wary of the strong tides that rip around the many crops of rocks surrounding the Tower. Any angler anchoring in the rocky regions here must use a grapple or rock anchor, as the seabed has claimed many an expensive anchor. Congers are the main quarry in the rocks, and the most experienced anglers from Eastbourne have a pocketful of individual rocks and marks around the Tower. During the late spring and summer months the spur-dog pack in this area, followed during summer and into autumn by the tope. For all these species, fish-strip baits are best, and most fishing needs to be with a wire trace for these big fish. In many places around the Tower, the sea breaks as white water over the rocks, and the careful, experienced angler who can safely troll or feather in these areas can hit good catches of pollack.

Many of Eastbourne's most popular and prolific marks are those further inshore than the Tower. One of the best known is the Horse, a large area of rocks running in a north-west – south-east direction about four miles off Eastbourne. It produces a great variety of species and some spectacular catches. Local anglers still talk of the day when a father and son – Fred Hearsey and his son Trevor – came back in their 14ft dinghy during a local festival with more than 300lb of conger on board from this mark. (Fred and Trevor are both members of the Eastbourne Working Men's Club). The Horse throws up plenty of white broken water when the tide is racing over the rocks, and pollack can be taken on feathers around it. In summer it yields good catches of black bream, huss, skate and conger, with cod added to the list in winter.

Level with the Horse mark, but further along the coast to the west, approximately off the Wish Tower – a landmark on the Eastbourne shore – is an area called Greenlands, which is a spur-dog hot spot in April. All the year round the mark is good for mixed fishing – especially for the larger species including huss, skate and tope. Another mark straight out from the Wish Tower but about 2½ miles inside Greenlands is the Copper Shoals, which is also well remembered by locals for a famous catch. During World War II Guy Read and a fellow Eastbourne Angling Association member returned from Copper Shoals with two common skate weighing 169lb and 133lb. Alas, local anglers reckon there are no such fish in the area nowadays. Its boulder, mud and sand combination bottom attracts a great variety of fish though, and rays and huss (with whiting and cod in winter) are taken, providing anglers fish the ebb tide, and especially the small tides. Further east and the same distance out lies another rock patch called Gullivers, which produces conger, huss and tope, and which also claims a fair number of anchors. Favourite baits for all these areas are mackerel strips – especially mackerel caught fresh as you fish during summer. Squid, herring and black lugworm are also used.

Small dinghies are used for flatfish work all along the inshore marks from 200yd out to about two miles from Eastbourne Pier eastwards, past Langney Point and into Pevensey Bay. The whole area is predominantly sand and mud, and plaice and sole are most often caught, although the numbers have thinned down now since commercial fishermen have worked heavily through the area.

Approximately half a mile out from Langney Point and half a mile east is the wreck of the *Barnhill*, which was a cargo vessel, machine-gunned by the enemy in World War II and grounded off the point. Fishing in the scour made in the seabed by the wreck produces plaice, dabs and sole, while good bass are taken during summer months around the wreck.

At the eastern end of Pevensey Bay, towards Cooden and beyond to Bexhill, there are several areas of rocky rough ground which provide pout, some congers and bass. These are the Coxsheath Shoals off Cooden, about 1½ miles offshore, also a whole range of rocky ledges and patches off Bexhill about the same distance offshore. Anglers fishing here are in strong competition with the commercial anglers who have been busy for many years. Inside these shoals, the same flatfish catches – mainly plaice – are taken right through to Bexhill. Most of the boats fishing this area travel west from Hastings, and many boats travel from Hastings as far west as the very rich marks off Eastbourne. Further offshore off Bexhill are the West Hards, which provide very mixed fishing over an area of rough ground and rock. Here, heavy tackle with wire traces will account for conger, huss, skate, tope, dogfish and pout.

The main boat fishing from Hastings centres around the wrecks that are accessible less than ten miles out. In the past few years, some of the potential of the wrecks has been decreased by demolition crews which have blown them up, but they are still a draw for big congers, pollack and bream in summer, with cod in winter. There is no doubt that some of the Hastings wrecks hold enormous congers, and some local anglers reckon that 100lb-plus eels live out there. Inside the wrecks there are marks off Hastings that provide mixed fishing for boat anglers.

About 1½ to 2 miles off Hastings Pier there is the Gulley, which accumulates all kinds of flatfish, with some good whiting in winter. Cod, which come into the Hastings area from October onwards, often last through winter until April. All the summer species – black bream, spur-dog packs, mackerel shoals, the tope chasing them, pollack and bass for trolling anglers, and thornbacks and plaice on the bottom – run through in larger numbers.

Much further inshore are the Castle Rocks, which are just visible at low tide. These provide good pout fishing, with a chance of conger and bass for anglers with even very small dinghies. Many anglers head east out of Hastings for the best inshore fishing, off the clifflands at Fairlight. A rocky ledge runs out from here, coupled with areas of rocks and individual large rocks all of which attract big bass, some congers, and whiting and a few cod in winter. Anglers fishing the area should keep a sharp look-out for the isolated single rocks that dot the area. Beyond Fairlight, boats out of Rye Harbour fish the big wrecks in deep water in Rye Bay. These wrecks – mostly all are at least six miles out – contain big congers, pollack, bream, pout and huss.

15 Beach and Pier Fishing

From Lyme Regis at the western boundary of Dorset to Rye at the eastern tip of Sussex there are more than 200 miles of beach, providing shore anglers with rich fishing. The Isle of Wight adds another 50 miles of first-class angling coastline with variety being its finest aspect. Dorset boasts the prolific Chesil Beach, which gives mixed fishing second to none in Britain, and the remainder of the Dorset coastline offers rock fishing in the same vein as that in the west country's rocky headlands. Hampshire's beaches support great numbers of flatfish – particularly flounders – and bass, both species being caught further east into Sussex. An additional attraction of the Sussex beaches is the chance of codling and cod during the winter.

Beach fishing is usually the newcomer's first encounter with the sea, so it will be useful to look at the personal gear and tackle needed. The top priority is to keep warm and dry and for winter this means wearing jumpers under waterproof gear with the added requirement that the angler must have freedom of his limbs for casting. As he is going to spend his whole trip at the water's edge – and step into the sea at least once during the day, wellington boots are essential. When fishing some of the Dorset bass beaches which have surf rolling in, thigh waders are necessary. It is important to keep the extremities warm, with a woollen hat to cover the ears and thick socks inside your boots.

The greatest factors in successful beach fishing are the choices of rod and reel, for the whole essence of the sport is good casting. To begin with, beach-casting rods are around 12ft to 13ft long, and a general-purpose beach caster will be sufficient to start fishing on any beach. As your experience increases or your preference for one particular species develops, more specialised rods might be required. For example, a powerful robust rod is

Two fighting cod taken by the author in his ten-foot rowing dinghy over a favourite mark off Lee-on-Solent. The bigger fish topped 13lb

(*above*) This 6lb 1oz bass came from just outside Weymouth harbour when the author was covering one of the Weymouth festivals there; (*below*) variety is the keyword of a deep hole off Lee-on-Solent. These two plaice (the bigger one topped 3lb) fell to the author in his row-boat last year

needed for rock fishing in Dorset, quite different to the spinning rod you would use to take mackerel from a shoal along a Solent beach, or the rod designed for long-casting to reach the codling from the East Sussex beaches. As your interest in the sport grows, making your own rods from blanks so that they are balanced to fit you precisely, or incorporate your own requirements – more or fewer rod rings, for example – is a whole new field of interest.

On the choice of reels, the beach angler is really restricted to two types, the multiplier and the fixed spool. For beginners, I would advocate that the fixed-spool reel – in which the line slips from the fixed drum – enables an immediate start on the sport with the minimum of heartache over tangles and bird's nests. The multiplier – which, it is true, will ultimately enable you to cast a greater distance – has a tendency to create bird's nests, as the line leaves a spinning drum, the speed of which can sometimes get out of control. It seems to me to be the common-sense attitude to begin with a fixed-spool reel, and progress to a multiplier when you find that the fish you are after are beyond the range of the fixed-spool reel. For much of the beach fishing in the area – from rocks in Dorset, for flounders on mudbanks throughout the south, and certainly from piers and jetties – long casting is not essential. Once again keep your tackle box comprehensively stocked. The south coast is subject to strong tides, and you will need a variety of the smaller range of weights. Fishing rocky or rough ground will lose you many sets of terminal tackle, so traces ready made up are a time-saver – especially during night fishing.

There are items of secondary equipment needed on beaches. These are a rod-rest, a landing net or gaff, and efficient lighting gear. The rod-rest is really essential, even if you are an angler who chooses to hold the rod the whole time. Each time you bait up, or wind in and clear away weed, or unhook fish, the rod-rest is needed to take the rod. At all costs avoid laying the rod down so that the reel comes into contact with the beach. There is no finer way to ruin a reel than by filling it with sand. Placing a rod on the beach nearly always chips the rod rings too. Rod-rests come in three basic forms – the monopod (or the spike), the bipod or the tripod. Spikes are one-legged rests into which the rod fits, with the rest as an extension of the rod into the beach.

These are becoming more popular for use on sand and shingle beaches. Bipods – two-legged rests – use the rod as a third leg for stability. Tripods – three-legged rests – are favourite for rocks, where spikes cannot be driven in, especially if the models with adjustable leg lengths for uneven surfaces are used. Of slightly less importance on beaches are landing nets or gaffs, unless you are specifically fishing for large species – conger or skate. The majority of fish taken – flatfish and bass – are small enough to land unaided. Fishing from rocks, piers or jetties, however, is quite a different proposition.

From a high rocky perch, any decent fish needs to be lifted by net, and in many cases a drop-net is more efficient than a landing net, no matter how long a handle you may devise. The drop from your fishing position to the water's surface from some piers may be even longer and drop-nets are then a must for landing big fish. It is nearly always necessary to get some assistance when using a drop-net. A helpful suggestion is to put a weight in the net itself to keep it steady and stop it blowing about. Drop-nets, which can be expensive to buy, can be made by fixing netting to the rim of a bicycle wheel.

While the rock fishing in Dorset is one of the area's best assets for the sea angler, it is also the most dangerous form of angling from the shore. Whereas the beginner can go straight to any beach and fish in safety – provided he keeps a wary eye on tide movements – there is no way a beginner should start his shore fishing from rocks. Rock fishing is definitely an aspect of the sport to graduate to after gaining a solid working knowledge on beaches beforehand. Often rocky headlands and promontories are reached only after climbing high and precarious rocks, and angling from the fishing platforms often means being balanced over a sheer drop into the sea. Rocks should never be approached at night unless you know their exact layout. Rock formations which are being fished at low states of the tide, and which are covered at high tide, will be extra slippery because of the seaweed on them. Making the sport even more dangerous is the sea, which is likely to produce powerful waves around rock formations, and which reserves its strongest tides for rocky spots. To help overcome the problems there are some golden rules. Never go rock-fishing alone. A companion can both assist in climbing rocks more safely and act as a messenger for help should an accident occur. Wear boots which will give you a positive grip – for example, leather boots with a grip-designed sole. Another safety-conscious tip is to carry as much terminal tackle as possible in your pockets, so that you can remain in your fishing spot and need not keep traversing the rock platform for more gear and bait every few minutes.

Between them Dorset, Hampshire, the Isle of Wight and Sussex sport about 20 piers, and hundreds of small breakwaters and jetties. Although all these piers produce some fish – mainly small flatfish, pollack and wrasse – none is included among Britain's top piers. Hastings Pier is probably the best, regularly producing specimen-sized plaice.

Piers fall into two categories, walled piers (or breakwaters) and piled piers (usually resort pleasure piers). The south has examples of both. It is harder to fish the breakwater types as stronger tides are experienced on them. The most difficult time of all is around high water – but that is often the most profitable period. It is almost certain you will need grip-leads to keep your tackle in front of you, and not tangling with that of your neighbour. Piers are prime examples where the angler must exercise responsibility. In the south, piers are favourite congregating points for holiday visitors, which can add to the difficulties.

Along the south coast bass, mullet, and wrasse can be taken from beneath the piles of some piers so it is not always a case of the furthest caster catching the best fish. If you do try to catch the fish 'under your feet' you must be alert to their speed and cunning in getting among the piles as soon as they are hooked.

Both pier fishing and rock fishing give the angler plenty of scope for float fishing, which accounts for large wrasse and pollack in Dorset, and a good mixed variety of species – pollack, bass, mackerel and flatfish – throughout the south, especially in summer.

Many of the south's sea-angling clubs cater especially for beach anglers and there is a great deal of benefit to be gained by joining one. Often clubs will lay on trips to away beaches giving you opportunities to widen your scope, which you would otherwise miss. Competitions always provoke two reactions. The dedicated private angler – who has turned to the sport to find peace and solitude – shuns them, while the angler who enjoys pitting his skills against others, revels in them. A new trend lately is for match groups to be formed. These are groups of anglers interested mainly in competitive fishing. They travel from one open competition to another, working as a team, bringing a team supply of various baits – dedicated to winning prizes. Nowadays, prizes can be very valuable at some of the larger festivals and open matches. The south coast stages some of the nation's biggest – the Hastings Festival, the Eastbourne Festival, the annual RNLI open staged by the Elmore Club at Lee-on-Solent, the Weymouth Festival and the Isle of Wight Open Festival. Televisions, radios, tackle vouchers of value up to £100, rods and reels are all regular prizes at the larger matches.

While open matches – open to all members of the public, club members or not – form part of the south coast club calendars, a greater part is played by internal club matches. Many clubs run them weekly or at least monthly, and it is here that a fairer reflection of an angler's skill is shown. Prizes are not won at the end of each match, but rather points are won towards the overall club championship. A concentrated effort is required throughout a season to win a club championship, and an angler's ability to catch various species as seasons change is tested. While match fishing serves in the short term to win awards, it has the benefit of improving your fishing techniques in the long run. There is no reason why your private pleasure fishing trips should not be the more profitable for using the knowledge you have gained in matches.

16 Chesil Beach and Portland Bill

Beach angling in Dorset centres around the twin attractions of Chesil Beach which is internationally famous for its mixed fishing – with bass, cod, spur-dog, skate, smoothhound, turbot, brill and more conventional beach-caught fish like pollack, pout and whiting – and Portland Bill – with its tremendous bass and conger eel fishing. Compared with these star attractions, the remainder of the coastline – particularly west of Chesil Beach (which means west of West Bay, Bridport) are rather ordinary fishing venues. In the extreme west at Lyme Regis, holiday-makers patronise the stone wall of the Cobb – the harbour – and catch small fish in summer – mainly pout, pollack, wrasse and occasionally mackerel, when shoals move through. Few large fish are taken.

Between Lyme Regis and West Bay (Bridport) there are two small fishing areas at Charmouth and Seatown. Charmouth has a sandy beach with rocky patches – and while it provides a shore-fishing venue, it also attracts the holiday-makers in their thousands. Often the only way to fish the beach is at night. Another way round the problem is to walk further to the east away from the popular beaches, until about two miles along towards Golden Cap where there are rocky patches to be fished, which produce some large fish, mainly conger, or even skate. On the other side of the enormous headland of Golden Cap lies Seatown, which hosts a beach-fishing venue sandwiched between the headlands on either side of the village. Anglers can expect to lose tackle in the snaggy rocks in this area and occasionally big fish – skate and huss – are taken with the smaller species of pout, wrasse, bass and dogfish. Further east along the coast towards West Bay Harbour is another beach set between two headlands at Eype. Once again the pattern is similar with rocky ground holding pout and dogfish, and with some big bass taken after dark. West Bay (Bridport) itself provides a double facility for anglers with the twin piers at the entrance to the Harbour, but fishing from them is very ordinary. Holiday-makers who flock to the East Pier in summer take small fish – pout, pollack, wrasse and bass, with some mackerel in summer.

From West Bay (the extreme western end of the Chesil Beach) fishing improves. Chesil Beach stretches for 17 miles to Portland, one vast unbroken shingle bank with deeply shelving sides, and with a kind of inshore lake inside it, leaving the beach itself as a narrow shingle strip with water on both sides. Because the steeply shelving shingle bank means deep water right into the beach, many species of fish usually reserved for the boat anglers are taken from here – hence its great popularity. Along its length, the major factor governing where anglers fish is the accessibility of the beach to the visiting anglers' cars. This has resulted in the twin villages of Abbotsbury and Bexington becoming well known as marks lying back from Chesil Beach, although there are very many equally good spots along its length for the angler prepared to walk a few miles.

Chesil Beach will have a heavy surf running most of the time, being fully exposed to the prevailing south-westerlies. It is also raked by fierce tides, and tackle needs to be strong with at least 25lb line and 6–8oz leads.

Because the variety of fish is so great, many anglers choose to fish with two-hook rigs (on paternoster or leger tackle) so that some experimentation with bait is possible. The ideal choice is to fish with ragworm, slipper limpet or small squid strip on one hook for the smaller species, with a larger bait (mackerel lask or larger squid piece) for the bigger species. Sometimes this becomes difficult to cast (although long-distance casting is not essential from Chesil) and less-experienced anglers may do quite well enough with single-hook gear. Chesil produces surprises throughout the year. In winter, pout and dogfish will be intermingled with good whiting and codling, and even cod running as big as 20lb. Squid bait, often cast as little as 30yd, will take the cod, which have been known as early as October, and which have lingered through the winter until the following March. Such catches are taken on either side of Abbotsbury or off the small village itself, where there are sand and shell areas, especially where the road runs past some fishermen's cottages.

Similar fishing rewards the angler from the Bexington marks further west and at Burton Bradstock which is still further west towards Bridport. Right through January the winter fish – boosted by the occasional pollack, brill, spur-dog, pout and turbot – continue to attract anglers. In the winter of 1976, Chesil produced a record-breaking 14lb-plus pollack and a record brill. But by February Chesil Beach, like most of the spots along the south, goes into its only decline of the year and it is April before the good fishing resumes – and that is the good news for bass enthusiasts. From April the earliest bass join the other fish off the beach – and they stay until December from some sections. From this time into midsummer the number of anglers visiting the beach begins to multiply. Black bream, red bream, pout, skate (mainly thornbacks), occasional turbot, and even congers join the bass off the beach, and as the height of the summer approaches and the mackerel are going well, it's shoulder-to-shoulder stuff along the beach. Shoals are clearly marked by the action of the gulls, feeding on the whitebait being herded along by the fish – and when they are in full cry, the mackerel themselves sometimes break the surface. Most anglers go for the mackerel with spinners heavy enough to provide the casting weight all in one – removing the chance of a tangle from a weight and separate trace carrying a lure or feathers.

At some points along the beach, congers are taken where there are rocky patches within range of the angler's cast, and he should always be prepared for things to happen that he would never expect elsewhere. Occasionally, packs of spur-dogs come in range and are caught. With enough big species possible, the angler should always have a gaff with him, and take heavy gear – including wire traces – in case he finds himself with something big around.

The conger mostly begin showing after May and June and they are taken most often off the beach at night. Burton Freshwater, immediately to the west of Burton Bradstock, is a typical place where rocks come within the range of the angler – and good congers over 30lb are the result. On long hot nights in summer, the angler with heavy gear will also take tope.

As the summer melts into autumn, the thornbacks become more numerous until October, and the later autumnal bass – while not quite so numerous – are bigger specimens. Flatfish anglers can also enjoy evening and night sole fishing during the autumn. Other flatfish enthusiasts who travel to Cogden Beach (midway between Bexington and Burton Bradstock) in summer especially at dead low tide, fish specifically for dabs with pleasing results.

There are two conditions when Chesil's night fishing improves. First is when summer nights coincide with a period of calm, or second, exactly the opposite – when a specially heavy surf is running after a blow has passed. About the only drawback to this is that large quantities of weed drift along the beach, which can be a menace. Chesil has one more surprise for any angler – and that is the occasional 'monster' which breaks up even the best prepared men. Most likely, these fish are monkfish or angler fish. If conditions deteriorate so that it is completely impossible to fish into the gale and surf, there is always the Fleet or Littlesea on the other side of the bank as a last resort. There are more bass, flatfish (mainly flounders) and some mullet to be had in these calmer waters. The best bass and flounder fishing is at the eastern Portland end near the outlet under Ferrybridge where the Fleet runs into Portland Harbour.

Immediately opposite this point on the seaward side is one of the best sections of Chesil Beach, mainly because it drops away even more sharply here than elsewhere, and even short-casting anglers can fish in waters over 20ft deep. They pick up bass and flounders, with codling and cod in winter – and they can also encounter the 'monsters' here which smash up anglers every season.

Portland Bill is the extension of Chesil Beach to the south – and fishing from its rocky fringes can be tremendous, provided your rock fishing is up to scratch. The very best Portland Bill fishing – big bass, large wrasse, terrific night congers – come from the most difficult and dangerous rocky sections of the Bill, where beginners or anglers not accustomed to rock fishing should never go. Portland Bill's tides rip around the rocks ferociously, the rocky points themselves are often precarious, and unless you have equipped yourself for climbing and rock fishing, and have mastered the techniques required, it is safest to stay away from these places. With Mother Nature constantly hammering the Bill – with men taking away other bits of stones, admittedly in nice, even shapes, leaving convenient platforms behind for the anglers – it is a rugged place, with many tons of rocks scattered beneath the rocky platforms above. No wonder there are many big fish among the rocks. With just two days left of 1976, one Portland Bill conger enthusiast, Jim Hadwin, took a 47lb conger from one of his favourite marks – and that's typical.

Mackerel fished on a wire trace takes the congers, while a slightly smaller mackerel bait to a long flowing nylon trace is likely to entice one of the big bass. Peeler crabs also account for big bass, and the soft-backs together with worms, will bring the wrasse out from the gullies under the rocks. Tackle losses here can be extremely heavy – and anyone who has once lost weights on a large scale to the rocks learns to follow the trick of the locals and use nuts and bolts as weights. If you are aiming at the big fish – and even cod to 20lb are taken in winter – a long-handled sturdy gaff is required. From up on the rock platforms, the holes and gullies between the rocks beneath you appear as white sections on a calm day.

For the visiting angler, the fun of catching fish from Portland without the dangers of balancing on precarious rock ledges can be had by angling from the more civilised section of the Bill near the lighthouse. But even here, your trip could become a nightmare unless you are geared up to expect to lose tackle in the rocks – or can change your methods to overcome the conditions. Remember that the tide will be racing so attach your weights with line slightly weaker than your main line and trace. Sparking plugs can be used as weights and if you snag on the rocks you only lose another piece of junk – not an expensive weight. Aim to be a little adventurous with baits – try peeler crabs instead of ragworm, or even strips of mackerel. With worms you would probably be limiting yourself to just wrasse – but with some bait variety you open the way for bass or even pollack.

17 Beach Fishing:
Weymouth to the Solent

From Weymouth as far as Hurst Spit's entrance to the West Solent, beach fishing in Dorset and Hampshire has variety as its keyword. Weymouth offers small species from its beaches; the 20 miles of rugged rocky coast between Weymouth Bay and St Alban's Head hold some of the best beach conger fishing in the country; and the Bay and headlands from Swanage through to Hurst offer sandy, muddy, rocky changing bottoms to complete the mixture with excellent bass spots, black bream venues and fine flatfish marks.

Weymouth's fishing begins on the north side of the Portland breakwater, where rocky structures still produce a snaggy area between the Portland breakwater and Weymouth's Stone Pier Breakwater. Bass, wrasse and pout are caught from this small cove, with bass and pollack coming from the breakwater itself. The inshore end of the breakwater – which guards the southern entrance to Weymouth Harbour – yields some flatfish and both marks produce whiting in winter. Night fishing for the angler prepared to use heavy wire traces and large baits will bring an occasional conger.

Around the sweep of Weymouth Bay the angler faces the incursion of thousands of holiday-makers by day, so that the only fishing possible is at dusk and night, bass fishing being favourite. Well round the bay lies a useful fishing beach beneath the picturesque Osmington Mills, where rocks, boulders and rocky ledges make good hunting grounds for bass, pout and bull huss. Once again, the angler who fishes big can take conger from this area.

Still further east along the coast is an even better area among the rocks of Ringstead Bay under an enormous headland. There is a convenient car park and a great variety for the angler – with

152

bass, pollack, huss, conger and even skate from the rocky broken ground with patches of sand between, and with wrasse from some of the marks inside the reefs. While ragworm bait might ensure a steady catch of wrasse and pout, the fishing is so good for bigger species that mackerel and squid can be used all the time.

Travelling east towards Lulworth Cove the angler is moving into the best possible conger country, save for one shingle bay at Durdle Door, where a greater variety of bass, dogfish and pout comes up. Congers can grow to between 25lb and 35lb along these rocky coastlines, and anglers perched on rocky outcrops can expect a mighty struggle from the first minute. To begin with, watch out for the conger gaining immediate assistance from the rocks around him. Two young anglers contacted my column to say that they had hit ten congers on a rock trip just west of Lulworth and landed four to 33lb. The other six had taken them straight into the rocks and smashed them up.

On the east point of Lulworth Cove itself (which is fabulously scenic) is another rocky area frequently exposed to the worst weather conditions, which provides good congers and bass. Once again, fish baits can be used to take them both. East of Lulworth Cove is Worbarrow Bay – which unfortunately for the beach angler is a gunnery range. You can fish the beaches in the bay only when the gunnery range is closed and you have permission to park your car short of the range and walk through. Red flags flying from St Alban's Head and Bindon Hill indicate that firing is in progress. Good-sized rays have come from the eastern end of the Bay towards the Worbarrow Tout headland, but the Bay is best known for catches of bass and pollack, with mackerel to be had spinning in summer. The gunnery ranges extend almost as far east as Kimmeridge Bay, which is an unspoiled quiet cove with excellent bass fishing mainly from its rocky ledges. The area is well blessed with supplies of peeler crabs which can be gathered from the rocky ridges at low tide, and these have a direct bearing on the good bass fishing, especially at night. While congers are not out of the question here, three-bearded rocklings are a more frequent catch.

Further east, immediately before the headland begins sweeping south to build up to St Alban's Head, lies a rocky bay under high clifflands, called Chapman's Pool. Careful searching around the Bay's rocky areas reveals several rock pools about 6ft deep which hold wrasse to 3lb. Ragworm is the best bait, and float fishing can be used when weather conditions are right. Occasionally float fishing will produce pollack. For the rest of Chapman's Pool, bass are caught regularly but the rocky bottom takes its fair toll of tackle.

St Alban's Head and its twin headland to the east, Durlston Head, are no places for easy beach fishing. Some marks are accessible to the angler, but only if he is a keen walker and fit. He can make his base at Worth Matravers, a small village on the Purbeck Peninsula. A small road leads down to Dancing Ledge where there is good black bream fishing in summer over rocks, while for the remainder of the year float-fishing techniques among the rocks yield pollack, wrasse, bass, with mackerel shoals coming in during the summer. Rounding Durlston Head and moving north the angler comes to Peveril Point, and from here on he has far greater access to the beaches and headlands. Peveril Point is a rocky ledge which produces the usual pollack and wrasse – with the additional bonus of bass for the angler using squid or mackerel lask.

Swanage Bay – beautifully sheltered from the prevailing winds by Peveril Point in the south and Ballard Point in the north – has a long sandy beach interrupted by groynes but does not produce very spectacular fishing. Flounder, plaice and occasional sole are caught, although it does improve towards the Ballard Point end where occasional thornback are caught. Once the beach ends and Ballard Point rises straight out of the sea, there is no access for shore anglers to the headland as far as Handfast Point and the Old Harry Rocks, so the angler's next vantage point is at Studland where he can fish Studland Bay. This is another sandy bay very similar to Swanage Bay and again is not very exciting for the beach angler. Flatfish are taken all along the Bay – mainly flounders and plaice – while the patchy areas of rock in range of the beach-caster yield a few bass.

Swanage is a good area for natural bait, with supplies of peeler crab, slipper limpet and razorfish on the biggest low tides. The razorfish live beneath keyhole-shaped holes in the sand and can be caught with salt. Pour a little salt into the hole and the razorfish will stick up a few inches. The trick is then to hold the razorfish still – do not pull it – and dig under it to lift it out. If you pull the section that pops up you will only pick up half of the shellfish. Some of Studland Bay's best flatfish fall to razorfish.

The first really good mark along this stretch of Dorset beach is at the Training Bank which is a continuation of Shell Haven Beach on the southern entrance to Poole Harbour. Where the man-made Training Bank leaves Shell Haven Beach the angler has the choice of fishing on the Studland Bay side or the Poole side into the Swash – the tide ebbing out of or flooding into Poole Harbour. Bass and flatfishing are both good along the Training Bank – especially with slipper limpet. Bass to 10lb have come from the Bank and the winter flounder fishing from it is excellent. All flatfish leaving Poole Harbour must travel through the Swash and casting into it is fruitful. Casting with sandeel and allowing them to work in the tide takes the best bass.

Across Poole Harbour entrance, the Poole Bay beach sweeps from Sandbanks, round to Bournemouth, with the two best marks being near Canford Cliffs and under Branksome Chine. Most anglers fish ragworm for flatfish – predominantly plaice – while bass and pout complete catches. All beaches along this area, from Poole Bay through Bournemouth and Southbourne, in summer suffer the problem of the presence by day of thousands of holiday-makers. As has been discovered elsewhere, the problem can be solved by fishing at night. One advantage of this is that in summer school bass often come within range of beach casting. Sole are the favourite flatfish along Bournemouth and Southbourne beaches with dabs and pout being taken.

Bournemouth beaches suffered a major setback in the mid 1970s as a result of having been built up by man. Fearing that the Bournemouth beach was being eroded too fast, sand and shingle dredged from deep-water marks were pumped on to the beach to build it up. This was carried out throughout 1975 and 1976 with the unfortunate result that all fishing was killed off. There is nothing in the imported sand and shingle dumped there to attract the fish, and nothing for them to feed on. Strangely, the one fish you can catch from Bournemouth is one you might want to forget. To begin with, baby pout often pester you until you become well practised at swinging in a small pout, grabbing it, unhooking it and throwing it back. Well, watch out for the weevers. Quite often they feed among the pout. You will notice the difference without me explaining it to you. The weever is the one that stings you with its spines and sort of sets your hand on fire!

Fishing improves towards Hengistbury Head, where there are rocks and where Hengistbury Head Groyne gives anglers a vantage point for fishing for bass, pollack, wrasse and occasionally congers. The Groyne, which has deep water on the western side and shallower water on the Christchurch side, lends itself to float fishing for these species if the weather is kind. Sometimes, float fishing here can be extended to include mullet fishing. Hengistbury's best fishing is reserved for those anglers prepared to experiment with baits like slipper limpet, live sandeels and razorfish. To the east of Hengistbury Head Groyne is a spit of land at right angles to the main run of the coast. This leads to the entrance to Christchurch Harbour. Across the narrow harbour lies Mudeford Spit, and both these areas produce bass and flatfish. A strong tide sweeps along these two spits which protect the harbour entrance, and some of the best fishing comes when the slack tide period coincides with sundown.

Beyond Mudeford, Avon Beach begins at Highcliffe and sweeps eastward round the arc of Christchurch Bay where good mixed fishing can be had. While plaice, flounders and sole make up the bulk of the catches together with bass there are occasional small rays. These come mostly at night (which is to the angler's advantage because the beaches are well crowded with holiday-makers by day). Lasks of mackerel or herring or razorfish will entice the skate. The bass last from April through to October in this area, with the bigger bass coming towards the latter part of the year. Immediately east of Highcliffe, beyond where the groynes finish, lies Chawton Bunny beach which also produces skate, bass and flatfish. Prospects for rays here are sufficiently good for a two-hook rig with 'double possibility' baits – ragworm and slipper limpet for flatfish on one hook, and razorfish, herring or mackerel for skate and bass on the other hook. High cliffs behind the beach along this stretch make access difficult but at Beckton immediately east of Barton-on-Sea there is good sole fishing during long summer evenings.

Further east, towards Milford-on-Sea, are the beaches at Taddiford and under Hordle Cliff, which are better still. The same two-hook trace used here can produce sole and plaice, with bass and more rays – plus the additional possibility of a conger or two at Taddiford. Silver eels are taken regularly along these beaches.

From Milford-on-Sea to Hurst Point is a 'mini Chesil Beach' complete with a thin highly banked strip of shingle (Hurst Beach) facing the prevailing south-westerlies, and with fairly deep water facing south-west. A fair variety of species are attracted to this beach starting with pout, dogfish, bass, flounders and plaice, but with a real chance of the bigger species like thornback rays and congers. Every summer seems to bring at least one sting ray and most winters produce a cod or two. To give yourself the maximum chance of taking the full variety of fish from here, be prepared to experiment with baits. Mackerel, herring, squid head, slipper limpet and ragworm have all taken fish here.

Piers

Weymouth Pier: This is a stone breakwater-type pier.

Swanage Pier: This is a short stone pier with very little to excite the angler who will find small pout and small wrasse pestering him most of the time. During the summer evenings black bream feed and pollack are taken occasionally.

Bournemouth Pier: Closed in November 1979 for major reconstruction work, the pier will be open for use again in the summer season of 1981, when sea angling will be catered for. This is an open-piled 'pleasure' pier which has some time restrictions imposed on anglers. It is closed after 10 pm in the summer months and after 5 pm during the winter. Summer fishing produces some variety with plaice, dabs, flounders and a few sole, with bass and a few pollack and with black bream, shoaling off the end of the pier within casting range. A few specialist anglers hunt the mullet, and conger enthusiasts who fish live pout under the piles have taken good eels. In winter, whiting, some codling and pout join the fish off the pier. Plaice can be taken until December but they then move off. By the time anglers begin catching them again in late February or early March, they are usually spent fish. Bournemouth Pier recognises that anglers are an integral part of the Pier's daily life by having a lower level all the way round for their convenience. This is of course closed in bad weather.

Boscombe Pier: This is a similarly constructed open-piled pier with the same fishing opportunities as its neighbour a few hundred yards to the west. Boscombe has better flatfish potential – except maybe for the dab – and its bass fishing is rewarding.

(*above*) West Bay (Bridport) Dorset: fishing from the eastern breakwater with the western twin in the background. Note the heavy swell swirling in between the piers – on quite a calm day; (*below*) a plump black bream of 3lb taken in the Princessa Shoal grounds off the eastern seaboard of the Isle of Wight

This 24lb tope gave the author good sport off the Isle of Wight – and then provided a tasty meal. Unless you are intending to eat your tope it is usually preferable to return them alive

18 Beach Fishing on the Isle of Wight

The Isle of Wight has nearly 50 miles of coastline all of which – with two exceptions – provide the beach angler with good sport. Mother Nature keeps him away from the stretch of beach on the south-west side of the Needles because the cliffs are too steep and the conditions too dangerous, and mankind keeps the angler away from the beaches in Osborne Bay, which are private. For the rest, the fishing is varied with good specimens regularly taken, and being an Island there is always a sheltered lee beach from which to fish no matter which way the wind blows, nor how strong.

The Island has six piers and is famous for its bass fishing from many venues and for its prolific ray catches – mainly painted rays – from the south-western beaches. Not surprisingly, competitive fishing has an enormous following and there are 20 clubs in the Island division of the National Federation of Sea Anglers, which is very active and which assists in the staging of several major festivals each year.

The westernmost point of the Island is at the Needles. From here to Cowes, the shoreline is, in effect, the southern shore of the West Solent. Although anglers cannot fish the Needles clifflands they can fish in Alum Bay, which has some snaggy rock patches which draw big fish. Big bass are taken for most of the year – predominantly from spring to autumn – and sole and conger are often taken at night. Alum Bay occasionally produces thornback rays and is one of the few Island spots where turbot are caught. Between Alum Bay and Totland Bay further east is the Hatherwood Point Headland which has rocks where the angler can take bass and conger. From here to Yarmouth – through Totland Bay, Colwell Bay, past Sconce Point and Norton beaches – summer and autumn produce the best fishing.

161

Bass and the invariable pout comprise nearly all the spring fishing, but by June sole are being taken at night, and they last until October, together with congers, pollack and dogfish from the rocky areas along the coast. In summer mackerel shoals come within range of the beach angler together with some bream and silver eels. Whiting and cod replace them during late autumn and winter.

Between Yarmouth and Newtown bass fishing remains good most of the year – only dropping off in winter, with Hamstead Ledge immediately west of Newtown being a top venue. This area produces some surprise big fish for summer anglers using mackerel, cuttlefish or squid. Spotted rays and a few thornbacks are taken and even an occasional sting ray has been landed. Remember this stretch of beach is immediately opposite the West Solent mainland shores where some of the best sting ray fishing in Britain – from Sowley and Lepe – takes place. Through summer and autumn, evening fishing produces sole, conger and dogfish. Spur-dogs have also been known from this area.

Thornback and sting ray fishing continues to be productive in summer further east along this coastline from Newtown through Thorness Bay to Gurnard. Bass fishing – together with the never-ending pout – is best during big tides at night when big bass can be caught on squid or cuttlefish. One Island angler who uses a different bait for bass is the NFSA Divisional Publicity Officer, Dick Hall, who has taken some beautiful Island bass, and who is one of many very successful specialists. He uses cheese for the Island bass on a special rig which has a treble hook as its secret. Dick uses a 4ft trace on a running leger through a very small weight. Sometimes when conditions are ideal, he can do away with weights all together; from piers and breakwaters, where cheese seems most effective, the weight of the cheese is often enough to sink it. The method is to mould cheese around the hook until it is completely covered. Other fish and crabs ignore it so if you get a bite, it will be the bass. Night summer fishing along this stretch of beach will also yield sole and dogfish, while silver eels add their brand of enjoyment. Mullet are also taken in June and July.

The West Solent ends at Cowes, and here the angler finds that his favourite summer fishing period is being shared by thousands of other people who flock to Cowes for sailing, holiday-making and touring. By day, its promenades and beaches are crammed, but at night there is more room for fishing – except in the first week in August which is Cowes Week (and on alternate years the Admiral's Cup Week for yachtsmen) when proms and beaches are crowded by night too. Bass fishing is good from Gurnard to Cowes from April through to October, and where rocky patches exist – including off the West Cowes promenade – good congers are sometimes taken. Across Cowes Harbour mouth, at East Cowes, the bass fishing continues, but the two esplanades at Cowes produce mainly small fish. Silver eels, some mullet, sole and mackerel are taken in summer with small pollack being an addition in autumn. While pout form the only regular winter fishing here, an occasional cod has been caught.

Beyond Old Castle Point at East Cowes lie the private beaches which are part of the Osborne Estate, originally connected with Queen Victoria and still having ties with the Royal family. The private beaches stretch beyond the inlet of King's Quay and almost to Wootton Creek. Angling recommences from in front of the holiday camp on the west side of Wootton Creek and from here eastwards past Ryde Pier to Puckpool Point flatfish hunting takes priority. Flounders are taken throughout the year, being at their best from April to September, with plaice fishing in spring and summer. Bass and pout are taken in good numbers with silver eels and mullet providing summer variety. An odd sting ray turns up along this stretch.

There seems to be slightly less variety of fish for the shore angler at the eastern end of the Island, with fishing from Seaview, through Priory Bay, past Bembridge, through Whitecliff Bay and down to Culver Cliff being mainly flatfish and bass (with the inevitable pout). Flounders provide the most consistent sport, being taken all year long. They are joined by plaice from about March through till August, and the bass start even later in the year, being caught only in summer and autumn. At Seaview particularly, and in Priory Bay, evening summer fishing sometimes produces big bass for an angler using large herring or mackerel bait. Node's Point at the southern extent of Priory Bay has rocky patches which yield bass, but a more popular mark is the old sea wall near the tumbledown church at St Helen's. Immediately south of it is the Duver, another longer sea wall which provides a comfortable casting position for bass anglers.

Beach fishing off Bembridge is a mixture of sandy fishing for flatfish with a few rocky areas for bass. Anglers who are careful to consult tide tables, and who can fish a rising tide during a summer evening, find the most productive sport. In Whitecliff Bay there is the extra variety of catching silver eels and some mullet from June through to August, but here the bass fishing is still favourite. When a southerly wind produces a surf in Whitecliff Bay the bass fishing improves noticeably. Under Culver Cliff lie rocks which produce small pollack. Beware of fierce tides which could cut you off in this area and consult local advice on the safety of fishing here before actually setting out.

South of Culver, through the wide arc of Sandown Bay past Shanklin and down to Horse Ledge, the fishing begins to improve with a far greater summer mixture. This stretch of beach is dominated by the two major holiday resorts of Sandown and Shanklin which cater for thousands of visitors. Beaches are impossibly crowded by day, but often the best bass fall to evening or night anglers. Double figure bass have come from this area. Redcliff, between Sandown and Culver, is probably the least crowded section of beach and summer nights sometimes yield conger while sole are taken in autumn. Just south of Sandown Pier is Lake Beach, which yields more big bass and where specialists use razorfish and slipper limpet to good advantage. Past Shanklin down to Horse Ledge, the summer variety increases with small pollack, shoals of mackerel and garfish adding to the potential. Occasionally a turbot or skate is taken in summer with painted rays lingering on as late as September.

Further south, past Luccombe Bay and Ventnor and along the southern shore to St Catherine's Point, beach angling becomes more rugged. Ventnor is a town of steep hills and most of the beaches around it have to be reached down hilly and steep paths. Fishing under Luccombe Chine, which can be reached by walking from the village, is also rugged, with patches of rock on which you can lose plenty of tackle, but which will give up congers as well as good bass. Congers are mainly taken in the summer, with the bass starting earlier. Dunnose Head lies south of Luccombe and from there westwards to St Catherine's Point there are very strong tides. Sandy stretches of beach off Bonchurch and Ventnor bring good plaice fishing in spring, while a few painted rays are taken. In summer this area yields a great variety of fish. Flatfish enthusiasts take plaice, sole and flounders, the rocky patches produce small pollack and congers, and painted rays are caught by the angler using sandeels or other fish bait. Immediately west of Ventnor, the beaches of Steephill Bay, which are a favourite draw for holiday-makers by day, are best fished for bass at night. Nearer St Catherine's Point is Puckaster Cove, one place where a winter codling makes a change from the invariable pout.

Most spectacular of the Island's beach fishing is the amazing mixed fishing in the south-west area, from St Catherine's Point to Freshwater Bay. These beaches face the main brunt of the heavy weather, and while most beaches cannot be fished during a gale they are tremendous immediately after a blow. A big surf hits the beach, there are many rocky areas with thick weed, and many big fish enjoy that combination.

Chale Bay, lying from St Catherine's Point to Atherfield Point, is renowned for its painted ray fishing. Anglers pick up the first rays in the spring and they stay throughout the summer and only begin falling off in autumn. They feed on sandeel, mackerel strip, cuttlefish or squid, and many long-casting experts who know their haunts take four or five each trip. Many of the rays are top specimens and, for example, the Western Wight Angling Club, which has bred a series of ray experts in the area, had 15 specimen painted ray medal winning fish in 1976 alone. But these are not the only fish from this area. Dogfish are caught throughout the year with a host of summer species − small pollack, shoals of mackerel, a few bream, occasional big fish like congers, tope and even turbot − coming in. A few thornback rays are taken during August and September, while codling and whiting join the ranks of the pout armies in winter.

The fishing which is available from Atherfield to Freshwater remains an excellent prospect, and sharks have even been seen quite close in along this stretch of beach. Painted rays are taken throughout this area while Compton and Brook Bays are renowned for their big bass, there also being other areas yielding double-figure fish. In summer, all the species found in Chale Bay are caught, together with mullet and bigger species like spur-dog, turbot, tope, pollack and even monkfish. Cod are sometimes caught quite early in autumn and last into winter when they are joined by whiting.

Piers

The Isle of Wight has six piers of use to the angler. Two, at Totland and Yarmouth, are in the south-western extremity of the West Solent; those at Sandown, Shanklin and Ventnor face the south-east; and Ryde Pier is probably the best known of all, being the arrival and departure point for the main passenger ferry service and being near two hovercraft terminal points of the Island's north-east shore.

Ryde Pier: From the angler's point of view the general popularity enjoyed by Ryde is a disadvantage as it becomes immensely busy during the summer season, notably with masses of people using the pier, but also with numbers of visiting steamers and boats. But it holds a great variety of fish. Flanked along its length by the Ryde sands, the Pier supports some first-class flatfish hunting for plaice, flounders and sole. Some of the best flatfish work is done nearer the shore end of the pier, where a few silver eels are also taken.

There is even wider scope for bass anglers. They can fish the pierhead – provided they remember the regulations that no fishing is permitted where boats actually berth – and if they move further along the pier towards the shore during high tide on summer evenings, large bass can be caught on ragworm. It is rather a shame that the pier is so busy during June and July as some of its most varied fishing comes at the height of summer, when shoal bass, shoals of small pollack and mackerel come within range of anglers casting spinners. At the same time black bream are caught around the pierhead in summer, seeming to prefer lugworm – an exception to most of the other species which take ragworm more readily. Soon after the bream arrive in summer the best of the pier's grey mullet fishing is to be had from July through to September. These again are taken mostly from around the pierhead and local specialists float fish bread paste a couple of feet off the bottom for them. Completing the list is the universal small pout which is taken in great numbers.

Sandown and Shanklin Piers: These produce similar results, with Sandown Pier – about two miles north of Shanklin – providing greater variety and likelihood of bigger species. Sandown Pier has the same bass, flatfish, mullet, pout and mackerel fishing as Ryde, but in summer a few garfish are taken among the mackerel. The real attraction of this pier is that in late spring and summer some painted rays and more rarely turbot and brill are caught. During late autumn and winter it is worth experimenting with slipper limpet from the pier as the plaice and bass (and naturally the pout) seem to prefer it to the overworked ragworm.

Shanklin Pier is not quite so consistent although all the smaller species can be caught in evening sessions. If an angler is prepared to try a large fish bait from the pier during summer evenings congers can be tempted, mainly from the landing-stage area. In contrast, the little fish caught regularly include rockling. In summer, mackerel shoals come within range and float fishing under the pier yields a few pollack.

Ventnor Pier: Further south is Ventnor Pier which is a favourite with anglers but which suffers the same problems as Ryde with large numbers of 'trippers'. Boat fishing is therefore during evenings and at night. There are rocks within the casting range of anglers on the pier – with one big rock being visible eastwards at low water. The rough ground around the pier attracts big pout, small pollack (with the best fish up to 3lb), a few congers and even dogfish. The sandy areas between the rocks produce plaice and sole – with sole feeding well during autumn evenings, and some painted rays. Mackerel shoals tempt spinning enthusiasts in summer while in winter, whiting and an odd codling are caught (together with more of those never-ending pout).

Totland Pier: The westernmost pier is at Totland extending into Totland Bay. It is not spectacular, but sole in autumn evenings and plaice, bass and pout are taken regularly. A few mackerel (that shoal so heavily further south off the Needles) come within spinning range, and it has produced a few big fish including congers, thornback rays and a rare cod. Pollack are taken up to 2lb. Island expert Dick Hall has pointed out that a surprise feature of this pier is that it sometimes yields edible crabs.

Yarmouth Pier: Totland's neighbour, about three miles north-east along the coast into the West Solent, has two surprises, in

Dick's experience. It yields edible crabs and lobsters. It also produces a greater variety of fish. Anglers fishing especially for bigger species with large fish baits have taken thornbacks and sting rays, dogfish and conger. In February 1977 I had reported to my column a spotted ray from the pier that was just an ounce short of the British shore-caught record qualifying weight. The regular species taken on all the piers − bass, pout, sole, plaice and mullet − are caught here. Spinning can produce mackerel when shoals move through, shoal bass and even small pollack. In winter, whiting and some cod come within range of the offshore section of the pier.

19 Beach Fishing round the Solent

The Solent's beaches are heavily fished by flatfish anglers throughout 30 miles or so of mainly sandy muddy and shingle beaches; by bass enthusiasts who find sport especially on the southern beaches of Portsmouth and Hayling Island; and by anglers who enjoy a greater variety of species from the West Solent shores. The Solent has Southampton at its centre, with its surrounding heavily populated suburbs from Totton in the west to Sholing and Woolston in the east. The eastern end of the Solent has Portsmouth with its surrounding neighbours of Gosport, Fareham, Havant and Waterlooville. These two areas alone mean that the number of potential sea anglers along the nearest available shores is enormous.

The popularity of the sport in this area is increasing, as shown by the ever-growing numbers of clubs, built on factory social clubs, working men's clubs and social clubs. Shore fishing here is seldom spectacular (except for the West Solent area with tope, conger, skate and even huge sting rays and angler fish) but the Solent's beaches are at least consistent. They yield flounders, bass, silver eels and pout and anglers regularly take plaice, sole and whiting in winter.

The Solent is renowned for its rag and lugworm grounds – existing from the western extremity inside Hurst Spit, through the rich grounds between Lepe and Calshot, with good supplies at Southampton, Hill Head and in Portsmouth, Langstone and Chichester Harbours, serving the anglers who fish Portsmouth and Hayling Island. The whole area is also rich in slipper limpet, especially after a heavy south-westerly gale when banks of slipper limpet are washed up on the eastern Solent beaches, Portsmouth and Hayling. These beaches regularly support large-scale festivals – with one, the Elmore Angling Club RNLI festival at

Lee-on-Solent, showing in the Guinness Book of Records as the largest single club beach festival in Britain. Beach anglers in the Solent have trickier-than-usual tide patterns to understand, with the stronger tides being found in the West Solent.

Hurst Point with its castle and lighthouse is a favourite beach, producing a variety of species in different conditions. Its greatest asset is the deep hole or Trap located south of the lighthouse, which holds a surprising mixture of large species – conger, skate, dogfish and tope. To reach the end of the Point the angler can walk – but it is more than a mile along Hurst shingle beach to reach it from the Milford-on-Sea end. Alternatively boats run to Hurst Point from Keyhaven just inside the Solent. In direct contrast to the deep hole is a sand spit not far away from it where bass feed, especially for those prepared to try peeler crabs rather than rely on the favourite lugworm. Flatfish anglers fish the sand on the north side of the Point where all four of the main flatfish species – flounders, plaice, dabs and sole – are caught, together with more bass.

In contrast to the heavily populated and built up areas of Southampton and Portsmouth, the Lymington area on the edge of the New Forest is thinly populated. But angling along these beaches is exciting, always with the chance of catching a big fish. It is one of the few areas where there are restrictions on fishing, as some beaches – especially east of Lymington – are privately owned. One of the most popular is Park Shore, renowned for its big fish. The beach itself is less than a mile long, but provides varied fishing throughout the year. At all times there are pout plus a likelihood of dogfish (not usually associated with beach angling elsewhere in the Solent), skate, and bass, with the summer additions of sting ray and tope and the autumn arrival of conger.

Along the next series of beaches across the Beaulieu river mouth, very long casting can be used to great advantage in chasing skate. On the eastern side of the Beaulieu river estuary lies Lepe Beach which can yield rich dividends for exponents of long casting with a large bait. A large mackerel or herring offering is the favourite for skate and this beach also produces bass, pout and flatfish. The skate potential exists round the corner from Lepe on the beaches of Stanswood Bay. Rounding Calshot Castle, and entering Southampton Water, the angler moves into the flatfish and bass dominions of the Solent. The west bank of Southampton Water is largely taken up by the enormous Esso Oil Refinery at Fawley and fishing is prohibited around its jetties and oil tanker unloading facilities. The first choice fishing mark along this beach is Hythe Pier which is a top bass spot. Night fishing is rewarding especially if you take the trouble to keep the ragworm bait moving on a long flowing trace. Flounders which are taken from dinghies above Hythe Pier can be caught float fishing from the pier itself.

On the eastern bank of Southampton Water the angler has a far greater scope – with flatfish as his main quarry. At Weston shore near Netley, flounders are taken in large numbers, with numerous clubs visiting this spot for matches. One useful technique here is to allow the tide to increase the movement of your bait. If necessary, cast with a weight slightly less than that required to hold your tackle on the bottom. In this way, allowing the tide to roll your bait in a slight arc downtide enables you to cover more ground and offers a more attractive bait to the fish. One regular hiding place for the flatfish along this beach is just below the seaward ends of the groynes. It is well to remember the rules of conservation along this stretch of beach as many small flounders are taken which should be returned. The same rule applies for the large numbers of school bass which feed along this beach. Similar flounder and bass fishing exists along the coast as far east as the mouth of the Hamble River, along the beach below Hamble Common.

One way to avoid the smaller flounders and pick out the bigger fish is to get away from the usual ragworm bait and fish slipper-limpet bunches or peeler crabs. Crabs themselves are a menace along this shore and the angler can be sure that if more than ten minutes have elapsed since any sign of a bite, his bait will likely be covered by a crab. The reason for the great popularity of the flounders is that they come in during the summer and remain into the winter, reaching their peak during late August and September. On the other side of the Hamble River the same flounder and bass combination is taken from Warsash Point at Hook, and for several miles along the beach to Hill Head. At Hill Head the bass fishing improves. One popular spot is the sea wall on the western side of Titchfield Haven. There are plenty of snags, boulders and short wooden groynes in this area which could cost you some tackle, but bass feed well over this ground.

Hill Head's excellent bait-digging potential assists the beach angler. Many anglers dig bait and stay on the bait grounds fishing for bass and flatfish after the tide comes in across the bait-digging holes. Others actually fish while they are bait digging. At low water, good bass can be taken off Hill Head by the angler in waders prepared to walk well out and who is then able to cast a further 120yd or so. Hill Head is the westernmost extremity of the area in which the big annual Elmore Angling Club RNLI Festival is fished. Most years the Hill Head section provides the winners — with big flounders and plaice having fallen to anglers using peeler crabs, and with good bass coming in each year. Pout and silver eels and small flatfish are caught all the way from Hill Head to Lee-on-Solent.

Most anglers can also enjoy evening sole fishing from the slipway at HMS *Daedalus* at Lee, although in the summer it becomes busy with water skiers who have a designated area not far off the beaches and who launch from the slip. By day the angler must beware of Royal Navy hovercraft which constantly use the slipway. Lee beach is a pleasant shingle and sand beach yielding flatfish and numerous pout throughout autumn and winter. Some of its best fishing is in front of the military firing ranges at Browndown.

Before venturing along this beach, which begins beyond the easternmost end of Lee's sea wall, anglers must ensure that the red flag is not flying. This indicates that firing is taking place and the beaches are the area where spent bullets fly. I once ignored the flag and literally became 'pinned down' on the beach. I finished up lying flat on the shingle under a small grass bank at the top of the beach while bullets ricocheting from target butts on the ranges kicked up stones around me and splashed into the sea where I had been fishing. Flatfish (mainly flounders and plaice), bass and pout are the reward of evening trips on this beach. On summer evenings mackerel shoals often work close in to the beach and come in range of shore casters. They sometimes swim in close enough to become trapped between groynes when anglers can make a good killing.

Browndown Beach stretches along to Gosport's beaches, the best of which is at Stokes Bay. This is a sandy, sweeping bay, with easy access by car, and with a series of car parks running almost on to the beach where you could nearly cast from the car.

Bass, flatfish and pout provide the main catches, but small black bream are taken in summer and occasional cod in winter. In December 1976 one angler took a 2lb sole and a 14lb cod in successive casts from the Bay and during the autumn of 1976 this stretch produced a strange surprise for two groups of anglers fishing a match. All the pout, flatfish and bass disappeared, and between them the anglers landed six fish – all red gurnard. Although red gurnard are sometimes taken by anglers spinning for mackerel in the Solent, this was a rare catch for the beach.

At the eastern end of the bay is the derelict and crumbling partly demolished pier, which cannot itself be fished but which attracts bass. Fishing near the pier, particularly from the eastern (Portsmouth) side, produces a few big bass. The south-eastern extremity of the Solent shore is Gilkicker Point, another favourite spot for bass – large fish falling mostly to anglers with long flowing traces. Tides are strong off the point and they increase the movement in a flowing trace.

Between Gilkicker Point and the entrance to Portsmouth Harbour is Haslar Sea Wall, another spot with easy access for anglers with cars. A road runs along the top of the wall with some access for parking. In places, the wall has a sheer, almost vertical drop into the sea at high tide, and as there are no barriers between the road and the wall, great care must be taken with parking – there have been fatal accidents in the past. At the base of the wall is a concrete ledge which is covered at high tide. Fishing is carried out from on the wall, from the ledge itself when it is exposed, and from the beach at lower states of the tide. Pout, wrasse and whiting are taken along its length with an occasional big bass and even an occasional winter cod. At the eastern end towards the HMS *Dolphin* submarine base, large mullet can be seen during summer evenings cruising beyond the concrete ledge, and they are occasionally landed. At intervals along the wall stone steps provide access to the beach, but anglers must take care when clambering up and down it as the lower sections are often slippery.

Across the entrance of Portsmouth Harbour are the beaches of Southsea – together with its two piers – and Eastney. While the main bulk of the fish are pout, flounders and small plaice, whiting in winter, small bream and school bass in summer, these beaches produce a few big fish every year – bass to 9lb, plaice

173

near the 5lb mark, and a few big cod every year are examples. Fishing from the two piers – Clarence and South Parade Pier – is not spectacular but both provide plenty of small fish. Pout, whiting in winter, small pollack, good silver eels, wrasse and bass are all taken from Clarence Pier – near the Portsmouth Harbour entrance, but there are distractions.

The whole of Southsea beach is an enormous holiday attraction and Clarence Pier is besieged in summer. The Isle of Wight hovercraft lands a few feet from the pier, pleasure steamers use it, and it carries the area's biggest fun fair. South Parade Pier, further east, similarly attracts massive numbers of holiday-makers. In 1974 the pier was substantially destroyed by fire but has since been rebuilt, and fishing is permitted during autumn and winter though not during peak holiday seasons in spring and summer. It produces small flatfish, pollack, pout and whiting, with some small wrasse and numerous tiny fish (rockling, weevers and blennies) which give sport for many children using it. Occasionally, in winter, big cod are taken and turbot even more rarely. One Reading visitor illustrated the value of local knowledge when he dropped into a Portsmouth tackle shop for bait during the winter and asked where he should fish. He was advised to fish from the pier, told what tackle to use, and where to cast. In 20 minutes he returned to the shop cradling a cod weighing 16lb which he had taken first cast!

Many anglers scorn the value of these two piers because they give only small fish, but they certainly do have a value. Early in 1977 there was a row about the closure of part of South Parade Pier to anglers which prompted a heartfelt response from some pensioners who would lose their sport. The greatest value of these piers that are not real 'angler's' piers is that they provide facilities for young children to enjoy sea angling before they have mastered the art of casting, and they afford comfortable fishing facilities for the elderly.

Between the two piers is Southsea Castle and the best flatfishing in the area is from beneath the Castle. This is an area of rocky ground with groynes and snags strewn about where good bass over 5lb are taken.

To the east of South Parade Pier the worst problems of over-crowding are encountered during the summer months and daytime fishing is quite impossible. Evening and night fishing produce bass and flatfish with bream in summer and whiting in winter. Not far from the pier itself, in line with Lumps Fort, beach anglers can cast to the innermost blocks of concrete forming the anti-submarine defence running out to Horse Sands Fort. The blocks (fished better by dinghy, see Chapter 12) provide good bass but long casting is needed to be effective. From the blocks to the West Winner Bank, guarding the entrance to Langstone Harbour, is a gently sloping sand and shingle beach that yields flatfish, pout and whiting in winter and silver eels, black bream and shoal bass in summer. Beach anglers fishing the West Winner itself, also take good flatfish and bass catches, especially in April and May when the plaice start to move in from the outer end of the bank. The whole stretch of beach at the eastern extremity of Eastney is easy to reach by car, and there are parking facilities along the front. Eastney beach has a large bank of shingle at the top which effectively cuts off the road from view, giving pleasant quiet fishing away from the crowds of Southsea.

Across the entrance to Langstone Harbour are the sandy, south-facing beaches of Hayling Island which provide bass and flatfish sport. The East Winner − Hayling's counterpart to the West Winner − provides similar good bass sport. All bass fishing at Hayling improves if there is a heavy wind-driven surf running, or if a surf is lingering on immediately after a gale has blown itself out. Hayling suffers from a holiday-maker problem, but not as acutely as Southsea.

At Gunner Point, at the western end of Hayling, the sandy beach is backed by sand dunes and a golf course, and some quiet, isolated fishing for bass is possible. Throughout its three or four miles of sandy, shingly beach Hayling produces bass and flatfish, mainly flounders and plaice, with slipper limpet a particularly good bait. It is a natural combination that the best time for gathering slipper limpet, immediately after a south-westerly gale, is the time when the bass feed on it most avariciously, and good bags can be taken. With careful timing after a blow and with a good surf running bass can be taken very close to the beach − in the first 10yd almost among the breaking waves. Flounders, pout and silver eels are also likely to be caught.

At Eastoke Point, the eastern extremity of Hayling Beach, better bass can be taken either on ragworm or slipper limpet, but the angler has two problems – the strong tides sweeping into and out of Chichester Harbour, and the busy boat traffic in the harbour entrance. During the summer, mackerel shoals often run through the harbour entrance in range of beach anglers on the Point.

20 Beach Fishing:
Chichester to Brighton

Beaches in Sussex from the Chichester side of the entrance to Chichester Harbour through to Black Rock at the eastern end of Brighton Beach are predominantly bass and flatfish territories, with some excellent bass marks along the way. One of the first is at the entrance to Chichester Harbour. Unfortunately, some of the best bass fishing in summer coincides with the heaviest boat traffic – many hundreds of yachts cruising and racing from the clubs inside the harbour, water skiers and motor boats including boat anglers. To beat the traffic, evening or early morning fishing from this sand spit are most profitable. Most anglers use king ragworm but more are learning the value of slipper limpet.

Between this spit and Selsey Bill, about six miles to the east, there is an unbroken sandy beach which attracts large numbers of swimmers to confound the beach angler by day. Bass feed all along this beach together with flounders and plaice. In autumn, evening trips produce sole and in winter, some whiting (usually rather small) are also taken. Bracklesham village about halfway along this beach has a car park; this area has been known to produce the occasional sting ray.

Selsey Bill provides slightly more variety with black bream in the summer, and some thornbacks taken by anglers using peeler crab. In winter, starting about October, whiting come in and a few cod swell the catches. Selsey Bill suffers in summer from being a collecting point for weed – not the dreaded Japanese variety, but the good old English weed. During May and June, and especially after a heavy blow from the prevailing south-west, great banks of weed mound up on the west side of the Bill. One bream trip there in 1976 provided two surprises when I found a hefty bull huss and a big grey mullet washed up in the weed banks about three groynes apart. One way to defeat the weed is to move round to the east side of the point, which escapes the heaviest loads. Bream and bass catches form the bulk of summer fishing from Selsey. East of Selsey beyond Pagham Harbour are shingle beaches which give pout and whiting in winter, flounders all the year round (especially for the angler capable of casting more than 100yd) and bass and bream in summer and autumn.

Beyond Pagham to the east is the holiday resort of Bognor Regis which has a sandy beach attracting thousands of holiday-makers by day, leaving the only worthwhile angling during evenings, night or early morning trips. All four species of flatfish are caught here together with bass, and whiting in winter. One useful bait which can be obtained by digging the Bognor mud is white (or silver) rag which come mostly when the angler is digging for lug. They are deadly for flounders and bass. Between Bognor and Littlehampton is Clymping Beach which is visited by heavy shoals of small school bass in summer. Portsmouth beach-casting specialist Ron Lambert tells the tale of fishing from Clymping when a shoal of bass was so thick they were bumping into his waders and he was literally kicking them out of the way to cast. At Littlehampton itself, most of the shore fishing is either jetty or tidal-river fishing. The nearest beaches fished regularly are at Rustington where there is shingle with sand down towards the low-water mark, which provides flatfish and bass fishing, especially for anglers using small red ragworm and slipper limpet. Further east along the coast at Goring, anglers can once again dig white rag; fishing after dark here sometimes produces mullet as well as flatfish.

The beaches from Worthing through Lancing to Shoreham are again mainly fished for flatfish and bass. Worthing has predominantly shallow water with gently shelving shingle beaches which attract flounders most of the year, beginning in spring. The summer months see the arrival of black bream, bass and mullet with golden grey mullet being taken. Evening fishing in the autumn months off Worthing produces sole, and all beach fishing improves with the onset of dusk. The regular catches of flatties and bass make Worthing beaches among the favourites for clubs staging open festivals. One problem during late summer and autumn gales is that the heavy winds blow up troublesome amounts of weed. Many of the flounders at

Worthing are small fish – the area once being described as a 'nursery school' for flatties. The bass and flatfish potential stretches to Shoreham where good catches are made from either side of the harbour entrance. Shoreham breakwater has also produced some cod and whiting as a winter bonus.

Brighton's beaches fish well for bass and flatfish if the angler is prepared to surrender the beaches to the thousands of holiday-makers in the daytime and fish by night, and is prepared to vary his baits. From the Southwick and Hove (western) end of the beaches through to the beach below the Blue Lagoon tackle shop, there are excellent night time flatfish and bass marks – with bass being taken up to 4lb. Although flounders are caught throughout most of the year, February and March are the best months. White rag is deadly bait off the Blue Lagoon beaches.

Further along the beach, before reaching West Pier, there are two flounder hot spots at Collonade Gardens and Holland Road. In 1976 for example one angler took 29 flounders on a visit to this beach. Plaice and dabs are also taken, with dabs showing better in the late 1970s than in previous years. Further east, past Brighton's two piers and before reaching the new enormous landmark of Brighton Marina, which already dwarfs all else along the sea front, is the Black Rock area which gives the beach angler a complete contrast. The rocky area begins off the eastern end of the promenade. The first secret in fishing it efficiently is to visit the area at low water and map out the bottom for patches between rocks and gulleys, which will be most profitable. Big bass are taken from this area, especially on peeler crab or on locally dug white rag. The Black Rock area is a source of peeler crab in the summer, especially between May and June. Occasionally conger and cod are taken in this area in winter.

Piers

Worthing Pier: This is a valuable fishing pier stretching about 300yd out to sea and is a favourite with mullet anglers. Their sport begins in June and continues through summer and autumn. Summer also sees the arrival of black bream, mainly from July until August; silver eels are caught at the same time. Moving on into winter, flounders, sole and whiting add to the sport. Although there are no restrictions for anglers on the pier they must only cast underhand as there is a safety precaution banning overhead casting. Anglers need not worry about this as most of the fish caught feed quite close to the pier. Many of the mullet anglers drawn to the pier – especially on calm days – fish light lines with a paternoster with droppers probably 1 and 2ft from the bottom. The best baits are the locally dug white rag, red river rag – or favourite of all, a cocktail of the two. On really calm days the mullet anglers float fish this gear and occasionally they also use bread flake. Standby baits include slipper limpet and lugworm for the other species caught off the pier. The favourite mullet and bass spot is on the pier's west side, near the landing stage, while the flatfish are mainly taken halfway along the pier on the opposite side.

West Pier, Brighton: This is now closed to anglers.

Palace Pier, Brighton: This offers a fair variety of species with its best fishing during autumn and winter. By then the fishing under the piles for mullet and bass which began in June is still lingering on, while flatfish, pout, whiting and occasional cod are adding to the sport. Some very big bass to 14lb have come from amid the piles under the pier, and the mullet anglers, with red river rag and bread flake, catch their quarry from June through till late August. In summer, shoals of mackerel come within range of the pier and sport is also had with garfish that follow the same pattern. Anglers fishing the piles for mullet and bass sometimes hit pollack, especially in summer.

21 Beach Fishing: Newhaven to Rye

East of Brighton there are sheer clifflands effectively creating a break until beach fishing is taken up with a vengeance again at Newhaven and all stations east. The exceptions under the cliffs are at Ovingdean and Peacehaven, both of which support some bass and flatfish fishing, the best being after dark. In winter, some codling are also taken.

Immediately to the east of Newhaven lies Seaford, which attracts large numbers of anglers and produces some tremendous fish – including a flounder to 4lb 8oz which has been claimed as the British Beach Record. Seaford has a promenade on which stands a pub called The Buckle which is a useful landmark – and a starting and stopping point to improve the fishing. A mile to the west of the pub are the Tide Mills, some ruins of old mill buildings standing near the railway sidings. This end of the promenade often remains less crowded than some of the nearer marks, and its fishing is better. From February and March onwards it yields big flounders and plaice.

A specially killing bait is a mixture of white rag and locally dug red river rag. Match specialist Brian Meades, who regularly takes good catches from this beach, passed on a couple of valuable tips with regard to this bait. Anglers using red river rag should always fish it on fine wire Aberdeen hooks. If you try threading any hook of a thicker design through these worms you will likely split and tear them. The fineness of the Aberdeen hook means that you can put these small worms on – sometimes up to eight at a time – and still leave them looking life-like.

Much harder to dig and difficult to find are the white (or silver) rag – especially the big fellows, lovingly referred to as 'snakes' by the locals in Sussex. Having obtained your 'snakes' there is no greater satisfaction than in finding a way to keep them alive.

Brian Meades has perfected this. You can keep them alive in sea water for as long as you like. He has the whole system well organised with a tank containing shingle and an aerator, and with this he keeps his 'snakes' for months on end. You can keep yours alive indefinitely provided you keep changing their water – a fresh bucketful from the sea about every third day. One word of warning is that the container you keep them in must *not* be tin; plastic or glass is fine, but tin is instant death to the worms. They must also be kept as cold as possible.

Back to the Tide Mills mark at Seaford – for those anglers who cannot get the two ragworm, they should find that lugworm in summer will be just as good a bait for the sole which come into this area. Moving east along the promenade to The Buckle itself, anglers will find that a rough rocky area yields congers on summer nights if a fish bait is offered. All along the promenade and further east to Splash Point there are flatfish and bass marks, once again best results coming for the angler using the favourite white and red rag cocktail. In winter the promenade offers itself in a new light, with codling, whiting, pout and dabs and still a few of those conger after dark. The codling usually come in during late October and the best fishing for them is after a southerly or south-westerly gale. While the locals usually take their best catches just before and just after high tide, the gulley off Splash Point can be fished at all states of the tide, and some codling are even taken at low water.

East of Seaford the clifflands are broken by the Cuckmere River and Haven (see Chapter 14) and further east between Cuckmere and Beachy Head is the Birling Gap – a favourite with bass and cod beach anglers. If anglers time their visits to this spot soon after low water, they can survey the ground and fish up tide – the most profitable time. The best mark is where the steps lead down the cliff at the foot of the Birling Gap Hotel. Rocks around the mark bring in good congers and fat pout. If anglers choose to fish the rocks – and they should only do so if experienced on slippery surfaces – they should beware of the tide rising behind them and cutting them off from the beach. One bait used here for conger and big bass is kipper. You need elasticated cotton to tie the kipper on (and if all else fails you can take it home for supper). In winter an occasional cod is taken from the Birling Gap on either squid, crab or black lugworm bait but the fairly good cod catches of the past are not so frequently repeated nowadays.

At Beachy Head itself, Sussex bass fishermen get very enthusiastic over what they consider the best bass ground in southern England. First, there is the mark known as the Sugar Loaf Rock at a point where steps lead down to the bottom of the cliff giving the angler access to vast areas of rocky coastline along to Beachy Head ledge. Immediately on the lighthouse side of the ledge is a mark called Felling Sands which yields tremendous bass fishing. Visiting anglers should heed one word of warning. If there is a big tide do not fish this area as you will get cut off as it rises. All the best bass fishing here is carried on after making a survey at low tide to see where the most likely marks are – and then fishing the tide up.

The first big bass come in during May and stay right through August, and sometimes the biggest bass are taken in September. Access to Falling Sands can be gained by going down the steps at Sugar Loaf Rock and taking quite a long walk along the beach, or walking along the cliff tops and descending the steps at Cow Gap. During low tide, searches between the Sugar Loaf Rock area and Beachy Head ledge should show the angler areas of flat ground devoid of weed and sandy patches between the rocks. The cream of the fishing comes two hours after low water and lasts until two hours after high tide. Undoubtedly the best baits here are the peeler crabs that can be gathered from the rocky patches from May through the summer. Fresh mackerel is a good stand-by bait and ragworm will also take bass. One bonus when fishing with mackerel is that congers will sometimes beat the bass to the bait. Three local Beachy Head bass specialists, 'Snowy' Russell, Richard Ford and Richard Harlow, have all landed congers during bass trips.

In winter the variety off the rocks increases, with some cod among the favourite quarries of anglers. Pout and dogfish with some whiting also brighten up the catches. Moving east from Beachy Head towards Eastbourne there are two more good bass marks which fish best at the same state of tide – two hours after low to two hours after high. The first of these is Fir Trees, half a mile west of the Wish Tower and in front of a prominent clump of fir trees. The bass in this area are at their best from June onwards. Further east, almost as far as the Wish Tower itself, is a mark between the second and third groynes to the west of the tower, immediately opposite Eastbourne's Grand Hotel.

There is little fruitful fishing from Eastbourne Promenade, but beyond the pier to the east are the Green Path and Langney Point areas, which are favourite winter spots. These marks are about three miles east of Eastbourne Pier, as the mackerel swims, and cover the area from Green Path across the beaches between the next ten groynes to Langney Point itself. In winter, the best whiting fishing of this whole area comes from here – especially with thin strips of herring as bait. There are also dabs in daytime, and codling and cod by night. This area comes into its own from November onwards and fishes well until January. Prime fishing times are from one hour after low water until two hours after the top. Another good bait here is the white rag which can be dug locally. Plaice and sole are taken in summer although catches are not so good lately since the area has been heavily netted and trawled in recent years.

Beyond Eastbourne are the Pevensey Bay beaches which draw great numbers of holiday-makers in summer and make fishing hopeless. But wait until after dark and you will get good flounder fishing together with whiting; cod can be taken in winter. Bass specialists who cast to the surf at low tide with white ragworm find good bass. These beaches yield some huge flounders; the secret is to cast a long distance using razorfish as bait. This area is blessed by having razorfish washed up on its beaches after a good blow – both the small razor shell (*ensis ensis*) which only grows to about 4in in length and is usually curved, and the pod razor (*ensis siliqua*) which grows to about 7in and which is straight. They are deadly bait used fresh (simply crack the small one in half and take out the shellfish bait, or cut open the pod razors and slice out the fish). They make excellent baits when frozen down, if it is done properly. Again it is a Brian Meades trick which pays off here. Shell the razorfish, lay them in a colander and pour boiling water over them. Dry them off and roll them in a newspaper, then seal in a plastic bag and deep freeze rapidly. When using them, razorfish can be made to stay on the hook by tying them on with elasticated cotton. They are used to the best advantage in February and March when the biggest flounders are caught.

Along Pevensey Bay beaches and further east to Cooden Beach approaching Bexhill, anglers also catch whiting and small cod in winter and occasionally a conger from the few scattered patches of rock along the bays. Norman Bay and Pevensey Bay beaches produce their cod between October and February when casting over 100yd is necessary. The favourite local bait aimed just at the cod is a black lugworm and squid cocktail.

At Bexhill itself the water off the gently shelving beach is shallow and long casting is essential. The best fishing comes from Glyne Gap which holds bass and flatfish in summer and continues the run of whiting and a few cod, in winter.

Beach fishing at St Leonards and Hastings improves with good bass and flatfish hunting, with increased variety in winter. Off the western end of the beaches at St Leonards one of the best marks is beneath the open-air swimming pool where there are gulleys in the sandy bottom and some rocky patches. White rag and lugworm take flatfish and bass in summer, while black lug takes whiting and cod in winter. The rocky patches extend as far eastward as Hastings Pier and give a chance of congers and pout. As with all the south coast holiday resorts Hastings is taken over by swimmers and sunbathers during summer days when fishing becomes nearly impossible. As often happens, the angler forced to fish at night to avoid the crowds finds the best fishing, which includes some very large sole.

About three quarters of a mile east of Hastings Pier lie Castle Rocks which are visible at low tide, and which attract beach casters. If you limit your fishing to two hours after low water until two hours after high water you will catch these rocks at their most fruitful. In winter they hold whiting, pout, flounders and dabs with an occasional visiting cod, while in summer they are home to bass, sole, plaice and flounders. Further east towards Fairlight the fishing consists of bass hunting from the rocky spots and dab catching from the sandy areas. Between Fairlight and Rye are good spots at Pett Level for collecting peeler crabs – and the beach here supports its own bass fishing and flattie hunting, especially for flounders and dabs. On the other side of Rye the bass and flatfish sport continues at Camber-on-Sea, where the beach is shallow but productive.

Piers

Newhaven Breakwaters: Newhaven's harbour entrance has two piers, the shorter East Pier and the longer West Pier – which is called the breakwater. Both of them are probably best known for their cod catches. The best time for cod at Newhaven is either during the tail end of a good winter blow or immediately after the gale has passed. Fish near the lighthouse end of the West breakwater immediately after high tide, with black lug or squid or a cocktail of the two. Remember that you are fishing here over a 20ft drop to sea level. Ideally it is best to fish in pairs, with one to land the other's fish. You must take a drop-net (easily made from the rim of a bicycle wheel) which needs to be weighted at its bottom to stop it blowing around the wall and to give you better control during the landing of a fish. In addition to the cod the two piers produce bass, dabs, flounders and pout with occasional congers just to test your drop-net drill!

Eastbourne Pier: There are plenty of small fish to be caught here, the standard of fishing being just below that of the local beaches – but there are large numbers of fish caught. Small pollack are busy around the pier's landing stage in summer, while specialists tempt out the mullet with bread flake and red and white ragworm cocktails. A fair selection of flatfish are taken, with sole during evening trips, and some big plaice during winter interspersed with dabs. Small bass (in summer and autumn) with codling and whiting (in winter) make up the quantity, even if the fishing lacks top quality. White rag 'snakes' are favourite baits here, together with peeler crab – and some new success has been met by anglers experimenting with live pout.

Hastings Pier: Probably one of the best sea-angling piers along the south, it has a landing stage which is invaluable, and even a facility for disabled anglers to fish from its top deck. It fishes well all the year round and has a deep gulley within range of long casters at its seaward end. In June, July and August the mullet fanatics go to the east side of the pier and float fish back into the piles for the mullet, using either bread flake or fresh fish flake (for example, a flake from a small pout). Other anglers, with white rag, hunt the pollack, which run to a rewarding 3lb, among the piles from the same landing stage. Although fishing is prohibited after 10 pm in summer, that is late enough for evening sole to show well. Large plaice have always been a feature of the pier, and in 1976 between October and December the dabs went mad, with more than one catch of over 30 dabs at a time.

Come the winter, the long-distance casting experts take cod and thornback rays from the seaward end in the deep gulley. Whiting and pout also feed there. In summer, this section of the pier provides good black bream fishing. At the same time shoals of mackerel come within casting range and a good number of garfish are caught. One secret here is to use a sliver of garfish flesh as bait.

Acknowledgements

My book could never have been written without the assistance of untold numbers of anglers, skippers, club and sea-angling-organization officials and friends, whose experiences form the backbone of the information on which I have drawn. I'm grateful to all of them for their help and advice.

Some angling experts and friends I pestered more persistently than others; I'd like to thank them for their patience and time, and for not getting fed up with me and my questions.

Those who suffered most were Steve Mills, of Gosport; Mike North, Vice-Chairman of the NFSA and its Wessex Division President; Peter Merritt, National Anglers' Council Sea-Angling Instructor, from Portsmouth; Brian Meades, of Sussex; Ron Lambert, of Portsmouth; Gordon Barfield, of Dorset; Steve Gathergood and Dave Elbourn, for their Solent help; Dave Adams, charter-skipper from Langstone Harbour and his many helpful fellow skippers; and Dick Murray, journalist and angling columnist of the *Daily Mail*.

Two other people helped make the book possible, and for whose help I shall always be grateful. Dave Morris, staff photograper of *The News*, Portsmouth, spent many an hour tracking along the south coast with me taking photographs, and Lesley Stephen spent many more hours hammering away at her typewriter helping me with the manuscripts. Without them I would never have made it.

Index

Numbers in *italics* refer to illustrations

189